Donnalnk Publications, L.L.C.

This Book Belongs To

OFF BALANCE
IN THE SPIN CYCLE

SHORT STORIES ABOUT
CONQUERING LIFE'S ADVERSITIES

2nd Spirit Books | DonnaInk Publications, L.L.C.

United States of America

OFF BALANCE
IN THE SPIN CYCLE

SHORT STORIES ABOUT
CONQUERING LIFE'S ADVERSITIES

BY CHRISTOPHER DUQUETTE

CHRISTOPHER DUQUETTE

2nd Spirit Books Imprint
Publishers Since 2012
An imprint of Donnalnk **Publications, L.L.C.**
601 McReynolds Street
Carthage, NC 28327

Copyright © 2020 by Christopher Duquette.

Donnalnk **Publications** supports copyright. Copyright creates a perceptive ethos, inspires the innovation of the written word, nurtures unique vision, and promotes free speech. Donnalnk **Publications** appreciates your purchase of an authorized edition of this book and for copyright law compliance by not reproducing, scanning, or distributing any part of this book in any form without prior written permission. In so doing, you support writers and Donnalnk **Publications** capability to publish books for every reader.

Library of Congress Cataloging-in-Publication.
Duquette, Christopher, author.
Title: "Off Balance In The Spin Cycle" / Mr. Christopher Duquette.
176 p. cm.
Subjects: BIO031000 - Biography & Autobiography / LGBT; BIO033000 - Biography & Autobiography / Performing Arts see Entertainment & Performing Arts; SOC064000 - Social Science / LGBT Studies / General; SOC064010 - Social Science / LGBT Studies / Bisexual Studies; SOC012000 - Social Science / LGBT Studies / Gay Studies; SOC017000 - Social Science / LGBT Studies / Lesbian Studies; SEL001000 - Self-Help / Addiction; SEL026000 - Self-Help / Substance Abuse & Addictions / General; SEL006000 - Self-Help / Substance Abuse & Addictions / Alcohol; SEL013000 - Self-Help / Substance Abuse & Addictions / Drugs.

Identifiers: ISBN – 13 - 978-1-947704-67-1 (alk. paper) | ISBN – 978-1-947704-42-8 (digital).

Printed in the United States of America
First Edition: 12 11 10 9 8 7 6 5 4 3 2 1; 2020. All Rights Reserved.

For more information contact:
Donnalnk Publications, L.L.C.
601 McReynolds St., Carthage, NC 28327
www.donnaink.com

OTHER BOOKS
BY CHRISTOPHER DUQUETTE

HOMO GOGO MAN: A Fairytale About A Boy Growing Up In Discoland

DRxug of Choice: Pick Your Poison

DEDICATION

I HAVE BEEN BEHOLDEN TO SOME imperceptible goddess who has been blessing me in circumstances I am willing to accept total responsibility regarding. My agnostic faith stymied me from researching and acknowledging exactly who this guardian angel may be. Perhaps with research, not a mystic palm, card, horoscope authority; I might get a vision of the world's history, like the *Holy Bible*, through a scientific perspective. I may discover a reference to a description of a goddess from an alternate culture, another human was able to discover, define and document, which will corroborate my own spiritual experience. I just know my blessed life has been due to protection and direction of some elemental of the female gender.

Being an attractive male, is a reality I have always benefitted from and an act I perfected to progress in the world, like a good movie star. In the past, in social settings, I became the best gay friend to the most attractive and self-protective women in every room. In revealing my homosexual orientation, immediately . . . in all social situations, women would flatter me and disclose their secrets in an unthreatened manner.

BINGO: I became the confidante of women in the room - I do not have this same emotional intimacy in my interaction with men. I fear misinterpretation of my intentions with me - so I keep an emotional and physical distance from heterosexual males.

And, then there is the male competition: who is the most attractive, best dressed, well-spoken, and well-developed musculature, which is like a pissing contest. I have conquered my innate low self-esteem defense mechanism thanks to group therapy that depends on honesty:

rehab, AA, private therapy, an unconditional relationship with my life partner Storm Orion, long-term friends, and my family.

This condition is not gender specific.

Women have the same social hurdle to clear.

This book is devoted to the women in my life who have instilled me with the confidence to reveal myself stark-naked.

TABLE OF CONTENTS

PREFACE

MOST EVERYONE IN MY SOCIAL NETWORK does not discuss the very personal, and unpleasant, contemporary subject of mortality, although we are constantly reminded the event is inevitable: whether by nuclear world war, deadly disease, fatal accident, projections of scientists or organized religions around the world who confidently forecast the inevitable apocalypse of human life on earth. I'm still undecided whether I want to witness the end of the world or not. If I do, hopefully it will be in the company of my loved ones because it would not be a monumental event if a few survive (nuclear holocaust) to share personal stories about the experience. It would just be how classic movies succinctly conclude with the legendary footnote: "The End." Not a fitting way to end a lifetime.

I wrote my first book, *HOMO GOGO MAN: A Fairytale About A Boy Who Grew Up In Discoland*, in December 2014, which was published by DonnaInk Publications, L.L.C. The title documents my actual experiences in experimenting and acquiring an addiction to the hedonism of discotheques and mind-altering substances, which enhanced, and masked, reality of the fatality of life outside the club. I might have danced under the mirrored disco ball too long. It was an addictive lifestyle I am fortunate to have survived after living many years in a nightmarish self-inflicted desecrated state.

After 5 years as one of my publisher's bestsellers, my first book seemed to satisfy a market interested in the past glory of decadent NYC. I was granted opportunity to flesh out the storyline through editorial and rewrites to achieve a more sophisticated, market-friendly, copy with a great new book cover, which invigorated promotions and attention for my virgin book. I am proud of the published 2nd edition now under 2nd Spirit Books, the Alternative / LGBTQ Imprint of DonnaInk Publications, L.L.C.; however, it was my 1st edition that was best-selling – so it had to be equally merit-worthy.

Additionally, my publisher gave me a green light to submit, and then publish the epilogue . . . my journal of 25 years addicted to the euphoric fantasy world of discos with the precursor of illicit mind-altering substances: *DRxug of Choice: Pick your Poison*, is the antithesis of my first book. By serendipity, it was published the same date as my 2nd edition of *HOMO GOGO MAN.*

While not as glamorous as the elitist attendance at exclusive high-end, underground clubs. In my early adulthood, I spent eight to twelve hours of every 24-hour day, dancing solo in the most transcendental body and soul occurrences I have ever experienced. This eradicated the busy commercial world outside the club's entrance.

The epilogue, going on 15 years, is based on avoidance behavior to overcome a financial and soul-breaking 'bottom.' I found myself com-mitted to the unglamorous world of keeping a multitude of appoint-ments in the waiting rooms of doctors and therapists, substance abuse rehabs, psych wards, emergency rooms, and pharmacies in the hum-bling company of what I knew were my psychological peers. However, I maintained an arrogant distance for the next 15 years after disco-theques were no longer in existence, coping with the aftermath of sub-stance addiction that controlled me in my 'disco' era.

Writing became a psychological handicraft.

This book, "Off Balance In The Spin Cycle" is a compilation of short stories of firsthand experiences I survived, with help from a silent and unacknowledged guardian angel I became aware of under undocu-mented experiences (dreams and near-death apparitions). The motiva-tion to present this book, written in 2020, at the advent of my home, NYC becoming declared epicenter for the Coronavirus (COVID19), making life in this formerly renown cultural, economic, and pleasure center of the world, a concentration camp.

COVID served up an insidious threat to the daily lifestyle those of us who believe we live in NYC, which to us is the *Land of Oz* where dreams have a better chance of becoming a reality without having to click a pair of red sequin pumps. This disturbing moment in history appears to me as our *World War III* with no human enemy to defeat with weaponry. This suppressive virus is beyond human capacity in the Art of War and resultant conquering.

I want to offer some of my experiences to readers that are both entertaining and depressing – like our current state of affairs. In moving through life, I never understood how I found myself in predicaments I did, that are now tales; nor, or how I survived them successfully.

Hope is the weapon I am equipped with to meet destiny. Hope for a better tomorrow as I purge myself of past discretions through a protagonist role in the expose' of my life's story. In the development of this title, I contacted characters from my 60-year storyline, with no agenda other than to make amends and revisit history. This book and my storytelling, in no way is meant to minimalize the seriousness of today's circumstances – only to proffer an escape from them and the anecdotal reality we overcome and survive.

However, in today's world, where a television spokesperson mentions applicating Aloe Vera are commonplace as measures of protection against COVID – I'm beset with dismay. This product I have lathered on my well-maintained body for years. It heals cuts and bruises, moisturizes fair complexions, and most recently, heals post-medicinal biopsies due to malignant melanomas, which I've been subject too. Subjected now to invasive scarring, I am reminded of the naïveté of self-centered tanning I engaged 25 years ago – just like the discos and drugs – payback to the devil.

Currently, I buy 24oz. bottles of Aloe Vera in volume online. And, I remain shocked and jealous I cannot acquire one of my dependable hygiene products locally because they are 'out of stock,' due to COVID.

So, I am 'now' in competition with newbies for Aloe Vera who prevent me from purchasing and acquiring my personal hygiene product at my favored markets. This is all due to a news spokesperson mentioning medicinal advantages of having the natural remedy as personal protection toward the virus.

Due to rants / vents such as this, I almost believe my egotism will present me and my work with an unflattering impression for readers; but I do not believe it is every man for himself. I can wait for Aloe Vera to return to local market shelves. I do not feel I am more entitled because it has been my product of choice rather than newbies doing everything to protect themselves – no one deserves this insidious virus and we all deserve Aloe Vera. Because once the product of 100% Aloe Vere became a well-known hand sanitizer for overly washed hands exposed to COVID-19, I realized my secret daily skin protection of decades was leaked by medical experts as a necessity. I had to suppress my entitlement. Everyone deserves to know and utilize the propensities of Aloe Vera. I was no longer entitled. I want everyone to benefit from the much-lauded medicinal aids of this ancient plant.

So, in addition to publishing two books under the progressive support of Donna**Ink** **Publications, L.L.C.** (www.donnaink.com) I am sharing this series of short stories I have developed over the past five years never thinking of them as more than a motivated story I share with an intimate network. Instead, today, I offer this title as a humorous take on the hubris of our out of control living. You'll sense some embroiled sarcasm amidst progressive politics, religion, and remorse.

This facelift transforms decadent memories of NYC and the 25 years I partied here (1976 -2004); and the unfortunate evolution of NYC from a land of opportunity to a commercial theme park targeted on the profitable tourist industry. NYC is no longer the magnet of talented and ambitious young adults that it was in my era. It is not the provider of friendly affordable neighborhood housing for grassroot native New Yorkers to call home, find career employment, and enjoy day and night culturalisms any longer.

However, my subversive memories of the decadent NYC will never be the same. They may have existed outside the scope of the former dreams of life in the Big Apple; regardless, I have hope and gratitude each day of life on earth, for something good someone did for me.

And, for what I can do to better the day of another human life on this Earth – I believe this work is worth it's test of time.

Pass it Forward.

INTRODUCTION

MARCH 2020: THE ADVENT OF THE unpredictably lethal Corona Virus has proven to be more destructive than when Godzilla battled King Kong in the aquatic harbor encircling lower Manhattan. The name of the virus, Corona, is not to be mistaken for the affordable Toyota Corolla, a Japanese automobile at the lowest sticker price of most luxurious automobiles offering the lowest standards of comfort and safety. But the resemblance in an alien name (Corolla/Corona) was easily mistaken by an ill-advised populace. The name of a car, like the name of a deadly virus, proved economically damaging to the Toyota Car manufacturing at the behest of the health crisis. An unfortunate circumstance. This could be said of the once promising federal departments in Washington DC. Staff appointed by expertise, not voted by the public, to oversee our populace's welfare with Economic Stimulus Benefits. The Corona virus will forever supersede the achievement of the Japanese Toyota Corolla, in reputation, and in its tally of fatal victims.

Living in the United States of America, in the most desirable metropolitan - known to never sleep - I was drawn to New York City at the ripe age of 18. Being full of the vim and vigor, I was anxious to explore the underground scene developing in the late 70's; driven by disco beats. Downtown was accommodating to those of us not interested, or financially resourceful enough, to spend time or money uptown. NYC, exciting and dangerous, offered a thriving existence and supported a multitude of social economic and cultural lifestyles.

Forty years later, there are no more desirable 'Manhattan' addresses. Rather, they are undesirable due to exorbitant costs in square footage. Today, 'desirable' addresses lay beyond the Island of Manhattan. Bordering boroughs once stigmatized as 'bridge and tunnel' are the new laissez-faire. New York City has matured and judgement free acceptance in all five boroughs has been achieved. The overcrowded city of the current hour has proven itself a receptive toxic swamp in response to the unidentifiable viral threat and our city draws on it like a magnet for where breeding young blood and desirable careers once took precedence.

When witnessing the destruction of the second World Trade Center from my Williamsburg waterfront rooftop loft on September 11, 2001, I was in the company of one of the more adverse cultures of the newly desirable bohemian neighborhoods. An orthodox Jewish man donned the strict costume of his tribe as the management representative for hip tenants, like me. We were the only two human beings at the time locked in emotions of shock, despair, and fear. We witnessed the 2nd WTD Tower implode while unidentifiable projectiles swarmed the sky, the moment was surreal - all too unpredictable - like life.

Tuesday morning of September 11, 2001, I was aroused out of bed at 9:00, way earlier then my late night and sleep meds would normally respond to. The unexpected apocalypse was the end of my progressively upscale NYC lifestyle. I worked the 800 square foot rustic loft with 12-foot high ceilings. I lived and paid the excessive rent monthly rent to call it mine. I discovered an underdeveloped commercial neighborhood held a multitude of opportunities. I had personal access to the rooftop with unobstructed views of East River from Downtown Brooklyn Bridge, Canal Street Bridge, and Williamsburg Bridge. These sights were easy to access (read no building permission requirements) for a desirable photo and video location. The south view from the three-story roof was unencumbered by any existing or future structure and an architectural monument to the classic ill-fated World Trade Towers.

My view included Empire State Building, Chrysler Building, and north as far as the United Nations Building. It did not require an official permit to rush a movie or fashion shoot from my off-the-grid residence without pissing neighbors off or involving nosy landlords. It was era classic.

Fast forward to current time, New York City has proven to be protected from any more sinister terrorists' insidiously prepared, massively destructive, attacks like those on the World Trade Centers. Now 20 years later, with a lot of money and loss of purpose, an ultra-modern skyscraper is constructed on the horrifically deadly site, which leaves no trace of the revulsion of it all. Exception being the surviving families' of 2000 victims trapped in the inferno and long-term medical aliments of those who escaped with their lives, those who risked rescuing injured, and those whose lifeless bodies were recoverable.

It is not the original WTC anymore.

EPIGRAPH

*"We should indeed keep calm in the face of difference
and live our lives in a state of inclusion
and wonder at the diversity of humanity."*

George Takei // Actor, Director, and Activist

OFF BALANCE IN THE SPIN CYCLE

SHORT STORIES ABOUT
CONQUERING LIFE'S ADVERSITIES

CHAPTER 1
'IT'S GOING TO BE A BUMPY RIDE'

Bette Davis's classic line from the movie 'All about Eve' (1951)

I GOT CLEAN AND SOBER IN 1995, after losing an undemanding job at a prominent public relations firm who produced campaigns for industries and citizens of high profile. We made millions $$$ by simply creating buzz words such as, "Just Say No."

In so doing, we enhanced the image of a contemporary imperial first lady cluelessly residing in the *White House - Nancy Reagan.* My dismissal from the firm was not due to downsizing or bad office performance; although even I knew, I was a bad office performer. I would take lunch in the local newly-minted restaurants of lower Park Avenue, which were geographically of no cognizance to the neighborhood of the PR firm I was employed by. I involved myself with co-workers and spent two hours drinking our lunch in these otherwise excellent food establishments in the resurrected historic neighborhood, like 'the *Old Tavern,*' once a speakeasy.

I'd return to the office alcoholically buzzed, page my cocaine dealer (BC: Before Cells) for the powder matter would wash my vodka cloud away and reignite my alcoholic pilot light pulling me back out at cocktail hour from my 9-5 job like a strong undertow. I'd then get lost in the deep dark sea of decadent New York City nightclubs open seven days a week and finally drown from party binging and pass out at 6am to wake at 8am for another workday and substance abuse tirade. It was hard to keep floating at this pace, but the hubris of my arrogant mind emboldened me to the routine day after day, week after week, year after year.

I learned the best night to party if one lived and worked in the city that never slept was Thursday, making Friday at work a difficult feat to muster. I drank, did drugs, and did not leave a club until the DJ started losing his muster and began playing old-school sleaze music (*Chaka Khan 'Clouds'* a favorite). On one Thursday night, my boyfriend, Tomas, and I took Ecstasy to enhance our experience at one of the most exclusive and irregularly scheduled parties for the most bazaar mix of club kids and social sophisticates. Susan Bartsch, a Belgian socialite of questionable pedigree had a knack for acquiring long vacant clubs we night-crawling nomads appreciated. These worn-out historical venues she acquired for single nights. We'd embrace the history, and not snub our noses at the wear and tear. We did not require an architecturally contemporary disco that was "In" until it was "Out" to love the nightlife.

This particular party was at the historic *Copacabana Night Club*. You could still imagine thugs and trophy dates bribing the Maître De for the best table for center stage entertainment. For Ms. Bartsch's grass roots party at the historic Copacabana, tables were cleared as the entertainment was elite attendees dancing to the best DJ in town. As we scuttled down the stairs to the subterranean dance floor, the infamous disco pop star Alicia Bridges was prevailing on the staircase landing. Spiky bleached hair, halter top, silver lame skin-tight jeans, and fuck-me heels, singing in a loop her one and only hit song: *I Like The Nightlife, I Love To Boogie*, then obsolete to her younger guests almost 20 years my junior.

I like the Nightlife

I love to Boogie

Under the Disco Ball......

I don't know how long Ms. Bridges had to sing this same silly dated song that night. It was like something you'd expect from a festivity of thriving party people who appreciate hiring their favored one-hit wonder to perform as if she were at Studio 54 twenty years earlier when her song was a commercial hit . . . now paid to impersonate herself like automatons at Disneyland.

As very late-night-crawlers, not leaving until the music stopped, Tomas and I returned to my newly acquired East Village Co-op some time before dawn. My boy-toy dropped to the bed sleeping like a baby and I wrestled with the speed portion of our Ecstasy trip. I was busily making calculations as to how many hours I could squeeze out of the alarm clock before having to get ready for work. As the sun rose through the eastern blinds, I realized I needed to cut the edge of the chemicals and my anxiety. Desperately I fostered a six-pack of tall cans of Budweiser from a 24-hour Bodega to keep me company during the end of my Thursday night diatribe. My boyfriend did not suffer the same party-insomnia as me. By 8:00am, I knew I was not in any condition to go to the office. I called and told the young, already on duty, staff member I was taking a much-needed sick day, but I had taken a lot of sick days during that calendar year.

Then, at 9:30am my pager went off indicating I had to call the office, when I dialed in – I was informed by the same staffer who I supervised, I was to report to the office. The messenger's voice was nervous. It was apparent he did not relish giving me, his boss, the message. I repeated I really needed a sick day as I was truly sick. The messenger's voice dropped to a whisper and he implored, "I am only following orders, you have to be in by 10:00am."

It was a fifteen-minute walk from my East Village Co-op to the Union Square office; this gave me no time to groom – still I mustered a shower, brushed my teeth profusely, and took a last final racehorse piss to empty five of the six tall boys I'd consumed. Then I woke and alerted Tomas it was time for him to go to his job while verbally expressing my panic that I might not get out of the unprofessional predicament alive.

It was 10am when I arrived at the office; I was met with eerie stony silence by normally gregarious security guards in the lobby. This ghost-ly shadow of doom continued as I walked down the hall to my office. I passed my boss's closed door and nodded at one of my drinking partners from the previous day's lunch. I checked in with my own small staff, both looked at me with nervous fear I detected in the phone call a half hour earlier; so, I retired to my office.

At the time, as System Manager for the successful computer room, I managed a staff of eight. My office was decorated with pieces of funky art, more than most managers in my profession would deem appropriate I believe. On the morning of my forecasted superseded sick day, I tried logging onto my computer, and it would not respond for me. It wa apparent I was locked out. Foolishly, I approached a female staff manager I assigned responsibility of account maintenance and she looked like as if was going to cry. She told me the man who had hired her for her job, me, was blacklisted from computer access. She was following orders from my boss and was terribly sorry.

Still, I wasn't sure what she had to be sorry about. My sense of entitlement permitted me to get drunk during a workday, have cocaine delivered to the office, and didn't permit me to believe I was getting terminated from my coveted job.

The fact my "sick day" was disrupted when I was instructed to appear at the office, albeit an hour after our 9:00am business day start, then locked out of accessing my computer by my own staff – still did not resonate with me. The act of preventing me from performing usual morning duties, given no indication by my otherwise loyal staff and co-workers as to what was going on, made me indignant. So, in Christopher fashion, I marched, still inebriated, down the hall to knock on my otherwise difficult to approach boss's door. Having been hired on my credentials, my immediate boss, the bald headed, dirty mustached, ill-dressed man I never got along with, was now instructing me to return to my office where I couldn't perform any regular duties. It was deplorable to me. I was instructed to just sit and wait for his call. I could never please my current boss. We were not a good match. And, his lack of tact, was making this ' *Twilight Zone*' morning all the more frustrating.

While quarantined to my funky office with nothing but the clock to pace my destiny against, what little alcohol was in my system to otherwise medicate me, evaporated quickly, and was replaced with anxiety. I sat in my silent office knowing I was about to be fired and was certain this was going to be due to the obvious truth I had a drinking problem interfering with my ability to function at the capacity my judgmental boss deemed acceptable.

My thoughts wandered. I wondered about how Alicia Bridges felt when she was paid for her gig the evening prior while portraying herself from her glory days for a party of people probably too young to even know or appreciate who or what she was at Studio 54 in 1980. My thoughts shifted to the professionalism I had in acquiring a progression of prestigious jobs in New York City as a fresh arrival from graduate school in 1981. This was to be the first time in my life I'd lose a job. The fact, I just HAD to see Alicia Bridges perform while on Ecstasy the night before, rather than get a good night sleep to arrive at work sober and on time seemed foolish in retrospect, as I sat there waiting my sentence.

I lost my indignation as I worried about how my career and future in New York was going to be destroyed. This humbled me from the otherwise charmed sense of entitlement, which fueled my career and reputation. My job seemed like a low-priority obligation next to my desire to drink, drug, love the nightlife, and, of course, my need to boogie.

Finally, I was called to the ugly boss's office. He asked me to close the door. With a very stern and disapproving look, he instructed me to sit. I was certain this meant I was being fired and possibly a slight intervention - if not a lecture - on how he saw my substance abuse adversely impacting my professionalism. The meeting was started by a third-party in his office . . . a representative from Human Resources. She offered the solace I was looking for.

I was told due to poor economic forecasts looming for the entire national business world, our company was downsizing. I was selected as part of the first wave of layoffs.

Still, I couldn't accept the thought I was no longer wanted by the firm. I directed a query to my boss first and then the Human Resource executive as to whether this was due to my attendance or the fact I tried to weasel my way out of coming to the office this very day; while my boss sat silent. I was assured by HR it was an economic decision. Even I knew I was overpaid for what little services I rendered the firm of late.

The company provided me with six months of full salary in severance to take time and evaluate my life, my career, my relationship, and my substance abuse. None of these topics were explicitly mention-ed in my layoff, but it was implicit to me. After Human Resources presented me with my severance package, I was escorted from the building as per protocol. Then I walked home from Union Square to my lower East Side home where I occupied and paid one-month's mortgage thus far. I was at risk of losing my first investment in real estate too. I never dreamed I would luck into the property in the first placed.

On my journey in a cascading downward spiral, of course, I stopped at a local liquor store to buy a bottle of bargain friendly generic vodka.

This reminded me of a morning I was rushing to my job in Union Square, where I witnessed a well-dressed thirty-something young businesswomen pushing her way through two vintage glass doors serving as entrance / exit for an established liquor store that featured a neon urine yellow sign electrifying the word 'Liquor.' Absorbed in the minutia, in a moment in time, in our city of millions, I'd noted the alco-holic cosmopolitan girl as she emerged from the lower Park Avenue Liquor store grabbing the neck of her bottle that wore an unfashionable brown paper disguise. When I'd taken the image in, it was as if I needed to report the details to some authority after something tragic happened to her. As if I were the last to see her in her high heels, with an attaché, shoulder purse, trench coat, and wisps of blonde hair flying lose around her face. If I had to describe her to concerned authorities the expression on her face would have been a combination of anger, shock, worry, and little satisfaction she obtained the medicine her emotions hungered at 9:00am. I assumed she'd already been to her office, received some upsetting and unsettling news regarding employment forecasts, and was unexpectedly heading home very early with a bottle of booze to keep her company her first day of unemployment . . . now, it was my turn to be subject to innocuous social interactions in the city of more dramas then all Broadway has ever produced.

I was home again with my alcoholic unemployment package. The generic vodka was laid on the counter alongside the overwhelmingly wordy printed legal severance package from my company. This was just as my boyfriend was preparing for his normal day at work. Our relationship was rocky. It was one of the last vestiges of my dignity. My well-paid professional job I no longer possessed kept us going. However, instead of tackling my new unemployment with a rolodex of loyal network contacts . . . I came home with my vodka bottle and immediately called my cocaine supplier challenging my drug addiction. This did not impress my much younger boyfriend as an activity of someone he once saw as a successful, dignified, disciplined older boyfriend poised to mentor him on how to impress, and progress, in NYC.

After having migrated to the pre-gentrified East Village . . . before the phenomena of the off-Broadway production of 'Rent' – I'd been offered opportunity to leave a small apartment in West Village. It had been a great place to live and notorious for offering the smallest apartments of any other desirable neighborhood after graduating from college in 1981. My new, East Village renovated apartment, was long and narrow, branded as a 'railroad flat' in real estate lingo. It was also in my price range and my first NYC real estate asset.

The pre-gentrified (read profit margin investors) offered me the comfort and bohemian appeal I felt like I was investing in at the perfect moment. I liked the neighborhood's acceptance of street art. One exclusive anonymous artist decorated lamp posts with broken dishes in a rustic mosaic pattern. This appealed to me. My newly renovated East Village co-op bathroom was outfitted with generic white fixtures, tiles, and walls, just like every other renovated co-op.

I got an idea to stylize the otherwise sterile space by visiting tile showrooms and buying a variety of obscure shaped white tiles. I placed them in ununiform jigsaw patterns grouting odd tiles along the wall and around the bathtub and noisy archaic water pipe. As usual, I was motivated by entitlement – I owned the space. I did not have to seek the approval of a managing agent or landlord and the escalating real estate market post-'Rent' was making my property an investment. I was inspired to perform renovations out of my own pocket to make the co-op remarkable in an otherwise uninspiring real-estate market. You might like my bathroom mosaics or hate them. But with an easy upgrade of cheap hollow wood doors to quality glass paneled doors, I frosted for privacy, while installing five of the co-op doors by an affordable craftsman made my railroad flat look like a more marketable (read: profitable) investment.

As I lay in a mess of grout and tiles on my bathroom floor – I drank and snorted coke. I was under the impression my contemporary avant-garde artist depended on inspiring me to make a mess that may never be appreciated by anyone but myself. I saw myself as a drug addled inspired bohemian artist in hiatus from my commitment to twenty years of slaving to the 9-to-5 corporate world.

Three months went by after the layoff. I made no effort to resume interviews for employment; however, I did buy a lot of cocaine and vodka. I kept up with bills, co-op mortgage and maintenance courtesy of the six-month severance package. My young Cuban boyfriend Tomas got his own place seven blocks away. Actually, I had never invited him to move in with me and relished my independence.

Now . . . I relished my irresponsible alcohol and drug fueled binges. I was put in the uncomfortable position to co-sign Tomas' lease on his own East Village apartment because he had no assets or credit scores ensuring the landlord he could pay $850 for a skinny one-bedroom flat, actually more like a studio, in a six-floor walk-up off First Avenue. I didn't have a job to satisfy the function of a backup asset to guarantee Tomas' timely monthly rent. Co-signing on a lease when I didn't even know what my economic prospects would be when severance ran out in three months was insane.

Tomas was excited about finally establishing his own place in NYC. I felt less like his boyfriend and more like his sugar daddy. I knew the apartment was his, but I felt like I had control over what went on in the apartment seeing as he could not have secured the lease without me. I was co-dependent on him. He was co-dependent on me. Without him in my life, without him as my boyfriend, I felt like nothing . . . seeing as I no longer had a job.

Cocaine and alcohol aside, I still wanted food, shelter, and a good-looking boyfriend to validate myself. Tomas invited me to stay overnight in his humble abode. When I tried to sleep on his thin futon mattress on the floor, I become restless, wanting to return to the comforts of my upgraded bed at home – causing tension when I left in the middle of the night.

One afternoon I thought I'd pay a surprise visit. Our apartments were only 5 blocks apart. Innocently, I rang his buzzer, sensing I was interrupting a secret rendezvous by the tension in his voice and response. He was caught off guard. I detected commotion on the other end of the intercom and felt entitled. I insisted I be buzzed in, to what I categorized as 'our' apartment. My paranoia was validated. I encountered a young hot stud (read: "slut") briskly passing me on the stairwell, averting eye contact with me. When I entered Tomas's love nest, I smelled incense, detected aromatherapy candles burning, and heard ambient music. This computed as not having been orchestrated for my surprise visit. I confronted my young lover with my suspicions, which were refuted and left the crime scene in a hissy fit. The writing was on the wall. My young lover was stepping out on me.

Tomas was interested in concert performances of his favorite pop stars. Reminder, he was 15 years younger than me. I preferred to avoid concert chaos by viewing an edited DVD if not just hearing a CD of the artist recorded in concert in the civilized comfort of my home. I suffered through my only visit to a live concert at Madison Square Garden to see George Michael perform at my boyfriend's bequest. Tomas acquired comp tickets to the George Michael performance from the star himself after he'd borrowed colored blazers to wear while performing from the Versace Boutique where Tomas worked.

George Michael's stage blazers were Mustard Yellow and Fire Engine Red with oversized shoulders. The complimentary seats he tipped Tomas in the Garden put us far from the stage, but my young lover found his way down to the stage pit while I restlessly performed my judgmental inventory on the audience of young teeny bopper girls. I did not want to be there, and definitely not abandoned, even as Tomas climbed back through the crowded stage area, up the mezzanine level, to reconnect with me in the top bleachers with a look of smitten puppy love on his face. Not for me, but for George Michael. We exited the stadium in silence with popcorn and Pepsi making a sticky tacky carpet all the more annoying on our exodus from New York's Class B stadium.

Nothing comes close to the historically well-maintained Radio City Music Hall.

I had a splitting headache and wanted to drink to obliterate the hellish experience. I swore I would never put myself in another event with the enormity of seating as the concert hall - sports arena of Madison Square Garden.

Four months after I lost my job, I had squandered four month's salary on nothing to evade the danger of losing my co-op in two more months. I was holed up performing the artwork in progress in my bathroom. Feverishly putting down time to crafty use by aggressively applying my now overstocked white tile supply to the walls, floors, tub, sink and water pipe in what I believed were unique and creative patterns. It is the end of a messy snow heavy winter in NYC and I relied on coke and vodka to spurn my creative juices.

Tomas, a big fan of Phyllis Hyman, secured tickets to the jazz singer turned disco diva . . . who I respect as a low down and humble artist struggling with demons like Billie Holliday . . . She was quietly scheduled to perform at 'the Village Gate' on Bleecker Street in the West Village. The Village Gate is an old legendary jazz venue in the basement of an odd mixed retail, cafe, restaurant, and poster shop on the ground and second floor of the historic West Village address. It was not on street level, making it an anonymous attraction to pedestrian traffic.

You have to be a jazz-aficionado to know where obscure 'Village Gate' was located. Just like fans of comedy know where the best off-beat Comedy Clubs are. Tomas secured the tickets on his own, which boded well for his proactive nature to drag our otherwise fragile relationship into a healthy forum of recreational and cultural entertainment. It would be something to talk about after Ms. Hyman committed suicide in a few years; our last chance to see her in the flesh.

Tomas comes to my apartment on a slushy snowy February night to find me graveling tile in the bathroom, quite loaded on booze and drugs. But we are to go out for a night of grand entertainment and adventure, so he does not berate me. He joins in on my party favors: coke and vodka. I clean and dress myself to respect Tomas' standard of appearance.

Even today, I always remember Michelle Pfeiffer's solo scene in 'Scarface,' as her coke anemic body sits at a luxurious vanity, to be interrupted by the reflection of herself in the mirror of honesty without a word of dialogue. The actress silently makes a most convincing portrayal she is not the trophy girlfriend of a Cuban-mafioso boyfriend, but a coke addicted skeleton. That was me. Once an innocent natural beauty selling his youth and looks for money, now close to middle-age, unemployed, and practiced narcissist trying to hang onto the last strings of a relationship with a highly desirable boy-toy influenced by the faux glamour of gay nightlife in NYC.

We dress as expected for a macho sophisticated gay couple traversing in a blizzard out on a Tuesday night to a cultural event. Heading out by foot to cross from the East Village to the West Village, no cabs available, we arrived at the Village Gate early enough to enjoy Phyllis Hyman's opening act. As we approached the venue, I noticed a large commercial passenger van with windows and overhead lights on spotlighting what I guess is a large drag queen making herself up with oversized hair like Chaka Khan in a stage sparkling gown with shoulder pads making her look like an NFL player. As we approach the entrance to the Village Gate, to secure our entrance to the club, I take a serious inspection of the otherwise private subject inside the commercial van parked on Bleecker Street in blizzard conditions and see Phyllis Hyman herself applying make-up to her beautiful face while teasing her hair with picks and hairspray. I wonder why she is not in the Village Gate's dressing room, but respect her decision to do it her way, as I always thought I did things my way.

I am a Taurus. Tomas is a Leo. No wonder we are attracted and distracted from each other. I don't know what horoscope sign Ms. Hyman is. I guess I could look it up on the Internet. She must be classified as one of the many suckers for sexual domination by men like Tomas (Leo) or myself (Taurus) who are star signs infamously warned in horoscopes to beware of. Other star signs may not present the initial burst of infatuation, but in the long run, are more about engaging with, emotionally and sexually.

Ms. Hyman must have been born under a star sign the persuaded her to end her life with a broken heart from a history of wrong star signs.

Tomas and I are in a comfortable dynamic for the night like it is the climax to our standard five years of no commitment (read: no legal but only an oral agreement). We splurge on cocktails while the odor of marijuana permeates the air around tables of mostly African American gentlemen and ladies presumably in the music business to rally around the star feature: Miss Phyllis Hyman.

She makes her way down center stage looking just as I witnessed her in the curbside van, only now she is in heels, which she immediately kicks off her feet and apologizes for presenting herself unprofessionally in her barefeet, defending her right to be comfortable at the Village Gate. A Diva. She sips hot tea on stage, explaining she is suffering from a cold and requests the audience refrain from smoking ANYTHING (pot, cigars, cigarettes) while she struggles to sing for us on this blustery night in this historical basement stage. Phyllis wins over Tomas, me, and the rest of the audience for an outstanding performance of human anguish, pain, talent, beauty, and sincerity.

After Ms. Hyman's final bow, Tomas and I visit the legendary piano bar and disco the 'Monster' on Sheridan Square, open seven days a week, to wrap up our night of debauchery and culture. We were having a good night. There would be bad nights ahead of us full of jealousy, judgment, and drama before we would both call it quits on the merry-go-round of our relationship, we dragged out for five years. I needed to set myself free of the relationship and get clean and sober to end the insanity I had contracted for but needed to break from. It was not Tomas, the NYC nightlife, drugs and alcohol, money; it was me.

After a weekend of binge clubbing and partying without Tomas, I was aware he was making his own rounds around town. I was informed by my night crawling resources who found it appropriate to contact me in the morning with details of Tomas's behavior and proclivities.

A favor or insulting?

I really did not want to hear any more, but I was addicted to the drama of my life, like the crack and cocaine. I came to my moment of reckoning on a Sunday when I acknowledged the reality of my unre-warding life: I was unemployed, my six month severance package was evaporating, and I was not happy with the results the self-subscribed treatment of cocaine and vodka I usually could rely on.

I had hit a wall.

I looked in the plethora of advertising in the back pages of H/X magazine - a free handout of gay events both good and bad in NYC. An ad for a rehab in Los Angeles for men like me who wanted to stop the party train, get respite from an insane life, and get clean and sober in sunny California called my name – I dialed their 800 number and explained my situation. Then gave my Cobra insurance information to an otherwise compassionate stranger and secured a bed in the LA rehab. The flight to transport my fragile surrendering body was being arranged by the rehab – as if I wasn't committed enough to make these otherwise responsible arrangements. I can't remember the name of the substance abuse facility that acquired my desperately unhappy temperament, but it sounded like paradise compared to my dungeon of hedonistic excess in the East Village I was finding to be a self-imposed prison cell. And, the photo image reflecting the epidemy of California in the ad was the deal breaker. Palm Trees not effected by seasonal change.

It was reasonably early enough on that Sunday night to call my otherwise out of the loop parents to confess my transgressions with D&A, and the action I had just taken. They applauded me.

My next call was to my first lover, Fernando, who had been my unethical case manager throughout this dark period of my life after 10 otherwise blissfully progressive goal-oriented years of living together. Fernando was an exceptional man who could help anyone, even me, the monster lover who had left him after ten years. He heard me out, took a breath and told me with his resources in the field of social work, he would make some calls on my behalf to find out if the LA rehab advertised in the back of a gay rag was really for me and what my alternatives were.

I did not call Tomas to help me. I called my ex who I had left for the Cuban boy-toy Tomas in my mid-life years (35 years old????) for help. Fernando helped me. He found the otherwise tony LA rehab I had committed myself to in the not best frame of mind was, in fact, the psych ward of a Los Angeles city hospital. I would be locked down. I would not be walking sandy beaches of Santa Monica at sunset or undeveloped parks and hills of Hollywood to get a taste of west coast serenity. I may as well stay in NYC and check into Bellevue Hospital. Fernando cancelled my scheduled trip and intake to the nasty LA prison I had orchestrated on my own naïve volition. It wasn't a rehab – it was a misleading advertisement for vulnerable drug addled men like me with H/X Magazine: a mixed bag of ads, escorts, and rehabs???

My sober and knowledgeable ex-lover (no longer a flight attendant but a PHD from prestigious Columbia University) sent me to the LGBT center on 13th Street in the West Village. I met a compassionate community services case manager who suggested given my situation: a secure home, ready to start applying and interviewing with an impressive resume in the computer industry, medical insurance, and desire to stop drinking and drugging - the only credentials needed to attend an Alcoholics Anonymous meeting - that I should participate in a long-term outpatient drug rehabilitation program on 23rd Street. This was only 17 blocks away from my First Avenue co-op I couldn't afford to lose. Like my life. Like my career. Like my family. Like my ex-lover Fernando and other supportive friends. Like my life in NYC.

However, I could afford to lose my Cuban Boy-Toy. Tomas hightailed it out of NYC after too much exposure (intimacy that equals being a slut). Fortunately, he retreated to his hometown of Miami. He blossomed as the face of the new South Beach Gianni Versace revolution ignited with the supplemental residency of Madonna. I inadvertently introduced him to her gay brother, Christopher Ciccone who thought he could provide more professional and social support than I - an ex-hustler/stripper who had gotten a graduate degree.

Back to me, I attended the daily group therapy sessions with a company of what I considered my peers from all walks of life at the 23rd Street out-patient rehabilitation center. The center is ironically associated with historical Bellevue Hospital across the street. I can't think of the name, I know it no longer exists, but I will always be grateful for the convenience and leniency to attend outpatient (live at home, check in and out like a job) as a freedom not provided by a rehab or structured living program. My comrades in arms were city bus drivers mandated to get sober and housewives who blacked out on wine. My racy story of the fast lane of drugs and clubs I believed my urban gay lifestyle demanded to be heard, not exploited. I was the only out gay client in the pack.

We shared stories with a professional Social Worker, educated with a Masters' Degree to qualify as a facilitator. Our group of newcomers sometimes did not recognize the boundaries of group protocol and interacted like normal humans during coffee breaks in the lounge. Inpatient recovery required attendees to commit to 28 days of structured and quarantined living. Outpatient permitted us to spend a workday at the facility, go home to our domicile, and commit to six months of daily treatment: 5 days a week the first month, 3 days a week the next two months, and once a week for the last 2 months including private counseling with an assigned case worker. Six months living free of structured quarantine is much more empowering then 28 days of rehab.

My case manager surprised me when he revealed he too was gay.

As an artist, the most distressing feature I see in the mirror – is my nose that I think is too big. Meeting myself with devaluation, my nose was actually in direct proportion to my otherwise handsome Scottish face. So much for self-deprecation and self-esteem issues in sobriety. I was not expecting this gratuity about how I viewed myself, considering how I had begun denigrating myself and my looks. Throughout my dramatic crash and burn from my choices of inappropriately young and beautiful BF's and voluntary commitment to a substance abuse program . . . this acknowledgement was encouraging information.

Today, I am very proud of my masculine nose and see it fits my face. It would sadden me if I submitted to cosmetic surgery to shave the distinctive overpowering contusion on my face. The unexpected lessons in bolstering your self-esteem from the honesty of recovery is refreshing.

Of course, I relapsed a few times.

On my first sober birthday, I felt I deserved to party on coke and alcohol. I projected I would just start counting days again. But I was honest in AA meetings about my sobriety only until I wanted to be honest. Besides, the few times I 'qualified' on my sponsor's behest, my honest story would be leaked from the AA rooms and be repeated to me at some party I would attend sober, with sober backup, by some stranger who I had never met but had heard about my sordid 'history.' Although the cocktail chatter was not from a member of AA, if seemed performing an honest qualification at an AA meeting was focused on satisfying your sponsor and things became Peyton Place gossip for most of the audience. So much for anonymity.

Once I secured a new job as an Office Automation Analyst at the then prosperous Republic National Bank, in a glimmering architectural wonder attached to an old limestone historic building on Fifth Avenue facing the NYC Public Library and the newly restored Bryant Park; I only attended AA meetings at lunch hour to listen and not share. Then I only revealed myself to a highly paid private therapist who told me I worked on my muscles too much. He said unless my occupation required me to lift heavy objects, there was no need for me to develop my muscles just for vanity's sake.

I had worked out on developing my muscular body since I was 13 years old, performing boot camp calisthenics in my family's basement TV room while I watched network television programs like the Partridge Family, the Brady Bunch, Love American Style, and all the Mary Tyler Moore spin offs: Phyllis, Rhoda, and the Betty White show. My therapist was an older gay man from another generation. He was doing his best to take me down from the pedestal I had put myself on when I became a narcissistic party boy. There was some truth there, but he did not understand fitness training was my religion, and probably saved my life from the amount of abuse my substance habit was wreaking havoc on.

With the help of my support group in AA, some very fine gay gentlemen with no agenda but to try and stay clean and sober, my therapy allowed me to search inside of the vessel of my sculpted body to look at my undernourished soul. My family unconditionally supported me. There was no help from the wacko gay men I dated and found out the disgusting true agendas they had (lies, sex, another notch on their bedpost . . . I got clean and sober for 5 years and six months before I threw it away when I met a charming, handsome, deceitful crystal meth head from a cultural background I had never conquered, but found fascinating. He, an Iranian from a privileged upbringing in Tehran who insisted on referring to his historical heritage as Persian, an empire that had not been in existence for 3000 years. He was also a Taurus, like me, who would never want to lose an argument.

Sobriety is a rocky road with life challenges that can't be anticipated or avoided.

Enjoy the bumpy ride.

CHAPTER 2
DOUBLE NICKELS, OR 55 TO STAY ALIVE

MY WRITING JUICES EBB AND FLOW unpredictably, a character-istic of the most highly regarded and unrewarded artists. But when they kick in, and I make the time to make writing a priority, I develop dexter-ousness arthritis from the momentum of hitting the laptop keyboard with the manic energy of Beethoven. My fingers become numb with throbbing discomfort like frost bite. This is not just from the common carpal tunnel syndrome, but self-induced butchering to both of my maj-or tendons after an ill researched suicide attempt the best neurosurgeon could not promise me any success in improvement to my dexterity.

After the guilt-ridden hiatus from my nocturnal industry of writing to be published . . . I got motivated to re-engage when I had already gone to bed after a long productive and exhausting day. I had already lost the wrestling match to succumb to the first wave of unconscious-ness produced chemically by Trazadone, the non-narcotic sleeping aid of choice for graduates of substance rehabs populated with a mixed demographic where I considered myself to be one of the anomalies.

After a successfully orchestrated discharge after a standard 28 days in the substance abuse facility, I was released to the custody of my responding father to reside in the mortgage free home he and my mother held in their retirement. Granting their demonstrative son, me, a room in a house I could live in with no legal restrictions. I was entitled: I had no legal charges outstanding, and an agreeable home environment living with blood parents who did not seem to display any absence of comfortability by providing a stable environment for me to call home after attending a daily recovery related schedule at an outpatient facility at no cost courtesy Medicaid, complete with transportation. I was grateful to my parents for their unconditional generosity, considering I left that very home under estranged circumstances (I was always acting out in activities and behavior I felt my parents did not make an effort to understand). The strong suite to my uncontested discharge from rehab to my parents' home as opposed to a structured living residence was that my father had been sober 30 years (20 in AA, and ten solo), and my mother was the queen hen of the local ALANON meetings, recognizing her attendance at this support group was not much then suffering through my father's increasingly daily consumption of alcohol than about her own feelings, and destiny. Not my father, but her. ALANON made my mother the magnetic attraction at any social function: Church, Red Hatter's society of cultural and pre-women's power, and of course, her evolvement to become more than the matriarch of our family, but an unconditionally ear to sound off to, regardless of generation, currently three, and with her DNA, probably strong enough to witness a fourth generation to our dynastic clan. Queen Mum.

So back to my artistic breakthrough. I recognize it is time to begin writing unfragmented thoughts that I have as I lay in bed intending to call it sleep time for my body and mind, but find the most alarming subconscious thoughts and curious storylines overcoming my ability to sleep. I don't want to miss out on these deep Freudian thoughts, so I get up, power up my laptop, put on some Paul Oakfield trance music on the lowest volume audible to my energized ears without disturbing the peace. I revisit some short stories I had started, left unedited and make footnotes to investigate (fact checking) of stories in progress, left unfinished at the part I last stopped at to remember to extrapolate on at a future date. That date is now. It was working. I'm motivated to resurrect these unrequited tales. I completed one short story I had started 8 months earlier to my satisfaction and embark on another fresh idea of fairytales.

I can only write so long before I crave for human interaction. So I step out of my apartment at 10:30pm to meet up with some friends who

I can count on being at a local watering holes, as well as meet new faces that are receptive to the collective hipster vibe at Schoutzi's Bar and Grill on Main Street, Poughkeepsie; a German beer garden-themed establishment catered to the more mature, sophisticated, professional, alcoholic and high-energy attitude that define "hipsters." I love the nightlife and order my tall glass of tap water saturated with fresh-cut cocktail-garnish fruit with a dash of a little sweet blue powdered pre-workout energy and focus substance that is the equivalent of 5 cups of coffee I keep in a small vial in my hipster man bag: Creatine. That's my drink of choice, and bartenders respect my choice as well as my tips to keep the window washer-fluid looking liquid topped off. Only a few haters suspect I am mixing crushed Mollies (today's Ecstasy) the loyal bartenders and owners of the bars and clubs I frequent are made well aware of my proclivities and are satisfied I am not doing anything illegal (I buy my product from GNC, on my Gold Card), and I have been regularly tested for high blood pressure and / or irregular heart rate, as well as learning moderation of my consumption unlike when I was an active alcoholic and drug addict. I always teetered the totter too much in one or the other direction: too drunk, too tweaked, too drunk, too tweaked, too drunk . . . etc. . . . .

My nights out at are fueled more by the vicarious influence of other happy party goers: their tequila, their pot, their coke high, and of course, the music from the DJ if he is playing something appeals to me. I also adore a good intense interview with a friend or stranger over anything they want to get intense about: politics, relationships, community services, sex, drugs, rock, and roll. I know when it is time for me to retreat from a conversation, from an establishment, or from the night when I can tell I am ready to go home to defuse, eat lightly, watch a DVD briefly in subtitles, brush my teeth, pull the blinds, unplug the phone, take a Trazadone, and tell a special someone who might be listening to me anywhere in the universe I am grateful for a good day, and now I would like a good night (minimum 7 hours) of restful sleep. Amen.

The next day might I wake up not motivated to go to the gym, which is usually how I schedule my highly productive week. I drink a protein shake, a Chobani Yogurt, peel a banana , bookended with two drags of an American Spirit Menthol light, brush my teeth, take note of the overcast skies and climbed back into my unmade bed for 3 more healthy hours of shut-eye and dreams. I wake up at 2pm to hear the cacophony of male voices shrieking and laughing like two Amazonian parrots in the wild wafting through my Levolor vertical blinds. I put on my oversized house boxers that are the equivalent of a nightgown, tip-toed out to my terrace surrounded by the protruding branches of a mighty oak tree, and look up two floors to see and hear a neighbor and a friend squawking like feisty yellow ducks who landed on another terrace. I produce a loud librarian "sssssshhhhh" to get their unguarded attention enough to be reprimanded by my seventh floor neighbor, Pacco, one of the two ducks, as he is celebrating his 55th birthday with Renato, the other duck, a tenant and constant influence on the building's esthetics (he's a theatrical interior designer) as well as a progressive influence on the apartment building's co-op board. Renato and his long-time lover / companion / partner Albin are like the couple from "La Cage aux Folles" with Renato playing the part of the gracious gentleman / manager of all affairs and Albin the more outrageous and artistic talent of the duo who can carry off a mean Carmen Maranda when he's not expensively coiffing women's hair. Pacco and Renato wave for me to come upstairs, in a come-as-you-are impromptu afternoon party on Pacco's terrace.

I've already brushed my teeth, I know my hair looks better fresh out the bed then after a shower (Pacco and Renato are awfully judgmental of my natural beauty), grab my cigarettes, cell, and Madonna's "B-Day Song" from her Molly-endorsing musical CD entitled MDMA (read: Ecstasy), which is actually a cool ditty of early girl-group sounding songs like the Go-Go's having fun with rock and roll while bouncing on beds like 6 year-olds. That's what I bring to a very spontaneous birthday party two flights up. A bright birthday song sung by a 55 year-old peroxide blond singer avoiding aging gracefully, Madonna, with shots of plumping fluids injected into her face to erase lines of character to serenade a 55 year-old Truman Capote-ish gay man who looks as good with his Italian olive skin as Sophia Loren did 50 years ago. Happy Birthday Pacco.

And the beat goes on...

I'm a happy girl.

It's my birthday song,

in a happy world.

I know it's going to be a good day.

Oh yeah, today is my birthday!

As the song completes its evolution (a non-melodic voice of middle-aged Madonna wishing "Happy Birthday" to small scatter of applause), a neighbor of Pacco's, Joletta, a late-seventies lonely old lady with tight curls ready to spring off her high-strung face yells down from her terrace one floor up that we are making too much noise on that Friday, 2:30pm, Secretarial Towers, Hudson Valley, New York. I turn the large black volume knob down of Pacco's high-end monochromatically flat-black stereo system half-way down, and Pacco assures

Joletta, who has already returned to her apartment, that we will be quieter and that, after all, it IS his birthday. TA-DAAAAH!

Mona Lake Jones, a college, business and fashion smart black girl with a feminine swagger like Queen Latifa, brings her heart of gold and a bottle of clear New Amsterdam Vodka, nes pas la make-up, topped by a cute street cap to cover her not yet styled raven locks. Mona Lake Jones is straight, ambitious, overly gay-friendly, happily hooked up to a nice Nubian prince, is between jobs, and ready to party with the boys in the band of Pacco's 55th birthday, as we all live in the same high maintenance high rise overlooking the scenic old Hudson River.

Rowina, another neighbor on Pacco's floor, comes out on her balcony to do who knows what. She is a sweet woman, so white and fragile she could be a rare, bleached albino creature. She does not respond to Pacco's megaphone voice calling to her either deaf or non-responsive ears as he says her name and bellows "hello." She either can't hear us two balconies away, or she does not want to engage with our high spirit of party revelry. Rowina just wants to attend to whatever she is doing on her terrace (maybe cleaning some dog poop off of her white canvas Ked's sneakers), and retreat to the privacy and air-conditioning of her humble abode. Pacco, Mona Lake Jones, Renato, and I are now once again left out on the seventh-floor balcony of Secretarial Towers at 3:00pm, to celebrate Pacco's 55th Birthday. I put on some mellower early disco music, 'The Best of Odyssey,' a 70's R&B Disco Soul group most famous for a sweet sad song about being young and struggling in NYC: "Native New Yorker."

You're no tramp,
but you're no lady.
Talking that sweet talk,
You're the heart and soul of New York City.

Taking subways,
making friends,
and finding lovers.

You're a Native New Yorker.
Nobody opens the door for a Native New Yorker.

Everyone is hungry. Mona Lake Jones orders Chinese to be delivered. She goes home to shower, set her face and hair, while I retreat to my fifth floor studio to play more upbeat music; the Tramps "That's Where the Happy People Go" which opens with a 60 second Liberace-like classical piano sonata intro before the company of brass horns trumpets in the song to it's easy jazz funky big band disco mantra:

Disco . . .
That's where the happy people go.
And they're just dancing along to a brand-new song,
Down at the Disco.
All my friends don't understand what's come over me.

When I ease on down, to the Disco.

I need to shower, shave, and perform some light grooming, before heading out of Secretarial Towers at 4:30pm to refill my one pack-a-week cigarette supply of American Eagle Menthol Lights, the politically and ecologically correct cigarette for those who want a healthier manufactured cigarette burns slow and long like a cigar, and encourages throwing cigarette butts in their proper place (no roadsides, no beaches) but in creative ashtrays they mail me regularly. I also want to bring to the birthday party a creative cheap alternative to a traditional birthday cake: a box of 8 chocolate-iced Entenmanns's baked donuts I will arrange on a black plate, tiered four layers, than 3, and topped the white trash cake with one rubber tires-like tires/donuts decorated with 10 tall thin 6-inch candles sparkle when lit. Always trying to be frugal and fantastic.

I return to Pacco's where the refreshed Mona Lake Jones is smoking a cigarette on the terrace with Renato, mixing Vodka and tonics for Pacco, Renato and herself. I have a club soda with pre-workout blue caffeine and herbs to enhance focus and energy and stamina in the gym and outside in my so-called life. I slip on a nice slow compilation by NYC's DJ Danny Tenaglia on Pacco's flat black stereo starts slow and moves up the grid in intensity, set the donut cake aside for after the Chinese takeout has arrived, and call my boyfriend, Storm Orion, in NYC to let him in on the spontaneous combustion taking place for Pacco's birthday. Pacco needs to be awoken by Mona Lake Jones as he was catching some ZZZZZZZ's in his bedroom, seeing as he started his birthday partying by himself and on the phone with the many friends and family members who adore him, starting at about 6:00am. To some of us, our birthday is still like Christmas morning.

I present Pacco with a personalized birthday card, something about good old friendships, and a sexy artistic and flattering photo of me taken 10 years ago, laying in the rushing waters of a stream feeding Lake Minnewaska, Ulster County, Hudson Valley, New York by a talented local photographer who always caught me in the right natural moment as I lay nude with my buffed body and Greek/Roman profile, worthy of either Playgirl (it was published with the intention of acquiring a homosexual audience, not for woman) or BlueBoy magazine (with model and quality production of Playboy magazine) or even the Metropolitan Museum of Art. The photo-grapher, Joe Puglasi, took a series of these nudes of me in a still chilly May 2003 as we were relaxed and secluded in Minnewaska State Park nestled in the historically protected Catskill Mountains in Ulster County. I was naked walking uninhibited though paths in forest until we got to the photographer's reason d'etre: a creek of rocky and photogenic water. I had been nude for long enough that plunging into this still icy remains from the surrounding Catskill mountains did not make me an ambitious muse. The freezing and dangerous waterfalls the photographer with an eye for nature knew how to direct me, until I got hypothermia from over-exposure to the elements and lack of food to offset the cream sherry, I drank prehab and today to stay warm and relaxed publicly nude. Joe Puglasi photographs other men in and under water, a memory from his early days swimming and succumbing to a lifeguard assisting him to shore from a strong undertow in Rockaway Beach, Brooklyn. He has an uncanny ability to capture men in and underwater, not as the featured image, but as an accessory to his passion of the beauty of nature and the shadows it casts rather than pigeonhole his craft from the populace of consumers of homoerotic photography. Joe was working his craft in the highly appraised and profitable world of stock art images. Joe's photo-graphic skills and my trust in him as an obsessive / compulsive photo-grapher always made me a good muse. I could follow his direction, knowing our professional repour would never prevent us from acquir-ing one in one hundred shots to satisfy his photographic sensibility, was grateful to be part of his marketable stock images, even if I was documented as nothing more than a coy fish in a pond.

The party ends after the shrimp rolls and BBQ pork are consumed (the non-Asian delivery boy was entranced in his destination drop-off party, and our overly generous tip). The sparkling candles were lit on the chocolate rubber tire-looking cake. I sang "Bon Anniversaire a Vous" to Pacco, and Mona Lake Jones and Renato

followed up with "you live in a zoo, you look like a monkey, and you smell like one too." Pacco made his secret sacred wish, blew out the difficult sparkling candles, and we all bit into parts of the chocolate donut cake. The party was over, and I needed to return to my home to make notes on this literary worthy short story 'Double Nickels, or 55 to Stay Alive.'

CHAPTER 3

THE NAME GAME

Madonna Fana Fo Fanna

Bo-ber-onna, bo-na-na fanna

Fo-fer-onna, fee fi mo-mer-onna, Madonna!

Come on ev'rybody, I say now let's play a game.

I betcha I can make a rhyme out of anybody's name.

The first letter of the name

I treat it like it wasn't there…

Lyrics originally sung by Shirley Ellis (1964)

Modified by Christopher Duquette

In Honor of Madonna's 60th Birthday

Born in 1958, the same year as me,

As were Michael Jackson and Prince,

I grieve they did not survive to see their 60th Birthday. RIP

EVERY GAY MAN WHO HAS LIVED in New York City, Miami, or Los Angeles, even a short stay in damp London, has a Madonna story to tell. It might have been a chance public sighting of the mysterious performer who has reinvented and reinvigorated the world as a provocative entertainer longer than the Beatles stayed together. But we gays are privy to inside information that tarnish Madonna's diminishing loyalty from her core audience because it is quite easy to see and hear accounts of her blatant-ly stealing fresh ideas from subversive society (LGBTQ, sexual revolution, censorship, spiritualism, S/M, politics, fashion) , repackaging them into slick videos and crowns herself the queen of these otherwise taboo subjects. It's not that she is an advocate for humanity, but a successful capitalist producing progressive and technically advanced concerts warrant the exorbitant ticket prices for a fan to see this aging one woman's show only Madonna can pull off. Hands down, the best live concerts produced, each new show surpassing the previous one as the star's ageing process requires more special effects to compensate for her diminishing human capabilities. Madonna will spare no expense to ensure her concerts are show-stoppers, and the audience is satisfied they got their money's worth. These fans who can justify the price even though they truly don't have the luxury of disposable income are devoted to this performer of four decades, and Madonna does not appear to be willing to retire, so she performs and builds her wealth on the captive paying concert audience (across our divided nation and around the not necessarily English comprehensive world). Herded into standing room only conditions for her notoriously delayed and overpriced concerts are her minions, like the babies she adopts. It is as insecure and cheap she does not share some of her wealth or a least announce credit for any inspiration or contribution on a project she performs with generous reciprocation. She prefers to reward herself as the sole benefactor she stamps with her ubiquitous name. But Madonna has been found guilty of plagiarism by the critics and well-read public opinion, and a lot of gays, as a lot of the well-informed public outraged by the unqualified dismissal of OJ Simpson. Madonna convinces the world she and her personal Giger counter discovered the yellow brick road of gold financial success. No credit to her street savvy backup dancers, dismiss-sed after one-world tour with no more wealth or credentials than before she employed and used them. "Paris is Burning" trumps "Vogue." If you listen to her lyrics, she is always repenting for her own hypocrisy. Power breeds greed, vice versa.

Celebrity power at Madonna's level can be more insidious than drugs to an addict. When confronted with disagreeable behavior, the accused superstar addict counterattacks, and there is no amicable consensus, just self-protective denial in her interviews. Another failed intervention. That so much of the inspiration for her always contemporary albums/concerts/images demonstrate her growing and financially feasible artistic potential are broad enough to satisfy her aging original audience and the new young fans not dismissing her for her seniority (60 years old; grandma's age!) with the best cosmetic surgeons on call 24/7 to ensure she's ready for the public's close-up scrutiny. That factor is not as important to the new blood attending to her product; it is Madonna's ear to the current young sound today's youth listens to attached to their high-definition earphones all day, and the all so important the young collaborators she has the advantage and power of approaching without ever being rejected. Young Madonna wrote and sang songs for a flailing rock band when she first stepped foot onto the gritty late 1970's stages and studios of NYC, where rags to riches dreams came true. Now she has cameo artists 30 years her junior contributing on her songs, so she doesn't have to embarrass her middle-aged (senior citizen?) damaged voice uttering youth street lingo or be accused of producing the basic 4 beats per measure pop becomes an ear worm tormenting you all day. Concert fans are now the financial cog keeping the music industry turning. The overhead that this businesswoman and sole attraction spends with no approval from financial suits to produce the most star-centric one woman show with undertrained but talented exotic sexy stage performers must be daunting and slightly undemocratic, not to mention the employment of the most respected and patient physical, spiritual, and cosmetic professionals treating the Queen Bee to keep her show ready. I know she has been advised a few times to give the blond peroxide a break, as her hair, as all blond addicts can attest, is submitting to a toxic treatment still not regulated by the FDA. Dancing in a slip with auburn bouncy curly shoulder length hair in a cemetery to the controversial 'Like a Prayer' was in my opinion her most honest expression of herself. Pepsi-Cola couldn't control Joan Crawford as CEO. They were still as cowardly to utilize Madonna's video to promote their synthetic soda.

So for an average young adult convinced they MUST experience a Madonna concert in their lifetime, it would probably require said college student to take a leave of absence from their State University for a semester to afford a Madonna concert ticket, not with VIP seating but to be herded into a standing room only stadium hoping to see the petite superstar make her grand entrance always no less than one hour late. Grace Jones used to spook her audience by opening her show with multiple transgender Grace look-alikes confusing and distracting from the real icon before finally presenting herself to the audience in the most dangerous methods. She sat on a large disco ball was lowered from the 30-foot apex of the Saint disco's atrium, shocking the audience as well as her entourage concerned of the risky entrance. Madonna is a spec on a large stage, lip-synching, recovering her strength and respire-tory stability from dancing and sometimes providing live vocals like a heart attack victim in ER as she ducks into the various foxholes conveniently scattered around the giant stage, allowing the exhausted perform-er to fall into a soft chair with waiting triage, sparing her the walk off the giant stage, past curtains, and numerous stagehands she has no energy to acknowledge, to be comforted and beautified like a much younger Dorothy before being royally introduced to the Wizard of Oz. Cost efficient, maybe spiritually and physically selfish about entitled lux-ury, as silent cosmetic and costume professionals perform the grooming to the one woman showcasing in record time, like inspecting, repairing, and ensuring a NASCAR is safely groomed before returning to the race track, Madonna presents a precision paced concert, in the limited time allotted after multiple dress rehearsals to ensure the show is perfect. Nobody would be the wiser if the DJ were signaled to mix fifteen extra seconds of music and video while stage dancers delay their performance to give the star more recovery time. Madonna might be small (by Alvin Ailey dance troupe standards) but has had to become mighty strong to direct her own shows to her level of perfection. Albums don't finance the artistry of the once novel music industry. Now it is well over a multiple of $100 bills for the bottom tier standing room only of her worldwide concerts she has never suggested retirement from.

Madonna has failed to achieve her broken dream of being recog-nized as an established actress; surprising how video-friendly she is. Marilyn Monroe got closer to breaking that glass ceiling of being a stage and movie thespian. But I felt Madonna humiliated herself to the elite politicians of Hollywood by advocating for her acting recognition in 'Evita' with full page ads in Variety 'For your Consideration,' paid for out of her own pocketbook. I've seen this fortunate and hardworking offspring of a struggling Detroit suburban family turn around her prospects to amount a fortune that is reported in financial journals as top tier for the past four decades. She's shrewd. And she'll cut you out of her life if her authority is threatened. An intimate open mike at the Sunset Boulevard Tower Records selected to broadcast Madonna live on MTV started late to promote her latest and edgy album "An American Life." The star was not ready, maybe because she had just learned to play the guitar that completed her new folk look, with no backup. Madonna lifelessly crossed the quiet stage, mumbled some sad folkish songs in a beatnik getup from her offbeat new album. A first live broadcast without the luxury of post-editing, and a flop. When an audience member requested "Like a Virgin" to maudlin Madonna, MTV production crews could not avoid the awkward and ugly response Madonna broadcast live as we all silently held our hopes and breath the star would do what stars are expected to do; entertain their fans democratically. But being the diva was in control at the moment. Madonna channeled the equally unprofessional and rude pit bull she can be, rejecting the request with an air disgust, as if a pair of lips with herpes and chlamydia sores were directing at kiss at her already fat injected lips. If it was as if Madonna's fear of STDs put "Like a Virgin" into another of the one naive audience members' mind to request. Mean Madonna muttered her hatred for the dated song, on air. Yet Madonna has prevailed worse scandals, divorces, a revealing tell-all book by her once soul mate and know estranged gay brother she entrusted with the role as her one-time unexperienced stage producer and artistic confidante. No explanation was ever given, other than family is not even a priority in Madonna's highly egocentric orbit.

At 60, she has to work harder to stay current to compete with the competition. The fickle music industry drives Madonna forward with advanced stage technology is a mask to distract the stressful dance performance this once natural dancer (actually accepted to train with the more street savvy dance companies, Alvin Alley) and was surprise-ingly honored with only one MTV video award for her simplistic dancing to the least complicated video she produced, 'Ray of Light,' which she modestly laughed as nothing more than a 40-year-old woman madly dancing like she's crazy. Amongst all the impressive portfolio of videos she has to her credit, even she expressed surprise the simplest in production value won her a long overdue MTV award. Loops of her missing a step during the live broadcast during a Super Bowl half-time show will haunt many viewers' ego, even hers, forever. In 1983, while my freshman college sister and I allowed black market speed to shut out the riot of a Saturday night at the Roxy Disco, my boyfriend breathlessly stopped our speed infested cackling to announce a white girl who can really dance was on a small stage lip-synching to artist's first radio hit, 'Holiday,' with two black backup dancers/singers, and he insisted we see this apparition for ourselves. We never would have guessed from the radio play this song was sung by a white girl, and she had the moves of someone with soul. My sister and I waved him away (a small stage performance while the club DJ was still playing for the massive dance floor crowd didn't seem like a life changing event). It was Madonna, in what was probably her first live performance of a hit song she toiled to get produced and distributed, using her feminine charm to get the up-and-coming DJ Jellybean Benitez from the Fun House Disco to play it as a favor. 'Holiday,' and all the songs on Madonna's introductory album, were hits. 'Borderline' will always evoke a particularly emotional moment in my life as I was having an affair on my devoted and broken-hearted life partner.

Public appearances seem to indicate Madonna has no fear of the bygone hourglass. Her ever evolving output of work embraces today's 20-year old raver who still takes MDMA to dance to tribal pots and pans club music (electronic music synthetically produced with minimal human vocals). Madonna's bread and butter, her impressive concerts, are for the young of body and soul, and a 60-year old ringleader has to muster a progressive sound to manipulates them. No more classics. It is the high tech, low talent, show stopping glitches that have also aroused resentment from the gay community. She shows no vulnerability. She still knows she relies heavily on the gays' approval to trickle down to the general public to maintain her popularity, stay in demand, and continue to be financially successful. She has alienated many gays in the music industry who gave her otherwise banal pop radio songs some panache once remixed and played in NYC dance clubs. Charm and ambition. But she famously does not like to give credit for ANYTHING or ANY IDEA for her artistry when it could help her aging originality to make her look less like some cosmic genius and more like a humble member of the human race. She may as well be a drag queen impersonating herself. Note: close-up selfies of a cosmetically fat injected face filling a smart phone screen on her 59th Birthday came off like a scary Halloween clown mask.

When I was in my post college 20's, birthdays were weeklong excuses for bad behavior, with alcoholic intoxication as an 18-year-old college freshman, threatening acute alcohol poisoning, dehydration, malnourishment, interacting with a well-intentioned Quaalude from a roommate would put me in a seriously dangerous state of unconsciousness. I was a narcissistic monster who always thought the world revolved around me, and I was undefeatable. When I hit 30, I was made aware of the uncanny fact I shared the same birth year,1958, as three of the largest pop icons of past and future decades: Madonna, Michael Jackson, and Prince. I wasn't necessarily a fan of any of these successful musicians separated at birth; I just didn't pay attention to the radio or read Billboard. I actually identified more with Anita Baker's attitude as to how and who hears her music, probably instilled with good DNA for being a perfectionist in her craft. She was a Taurus born in 1958.

I heard the melody of disco music in dark drugged underground clubs, and never bothered to follow the lyrics. Musicians even admit to garbling lyrics while f**ked up in recording studios, so lyrics are what you want to make of them. I need a beat so I can move my hips that set the metronome of my dance beat. I've got Latin blood, and the rest of the body follows like jellyfish tentacles. Dark clubs, anonymity, a crowd rather than a single dance partner to dance with, and no self-consciousness of mirrored walls, and no romantic notion of cruising for love with the "sex dance." That's a total distraction from my mantra to achieve the euphoria of dance. It was a performance in clubs like Studio 54, but it is the soul-searching experience in downtown underground clubs where the disco bug bit me. Before endorphin highs from lifting weights, now I would spend every Saturday night for hours (1 – 8?) dancing to the discovery of DJ-mixed disco music. That was my Nirvana.

I always needed a new song for my burlesque performance as a stripper at the Gaiety Male Theater, and with no costumes or props, so I relied on the chill that a good disco song could electrify my nervous system when in private clubs dancing not for money but for the profit of my soul. That and some poppers. Peter Brown's "Do You Wanna Get Funky with Me?" took control of my attention as my next new perform-ance, an innocent college student, into the inferno of hell. I performed to the song, not for the audience at the Gaiety for pay, but at under-ground clubs for the darkness of the song that I could feel with no other human attention or validation.

I was proud to provide 1958 as my birth year, even though father time keeps me looking like I was born in 1980. Good genes, procras-tinating visits to the gym to utilize ergonomically designed machines (no more free weights) and good facial hygiene (retinol).

Aside from Madonna's long play remixes (hate albums containing one desirable song that fills the rest of the album's playlist with wasteful tracks), I prefer 70's R&B musicians who could give me the beat to dance with the rhythm on 12-inch-long play singles: the Original's "Down to Love Town," Thelma Houston "Don't leave me this Way," Kool and the Gang's "Get down with the Genie," Double Exposure's "Ten Percent of Nothing," Diana Ross's "Love Hangover."

I still buy Madonna albums, hate them at first, appreciate the amount of work involved on a second listen, and buy DVDs of her con-cert performances I refuse to attend due to my inability to squander unaffordable tickets, or be in a riotous stadium. I admire her ability to milk her audience to be on demanding frequency for two hours as she shuffles through greatly orchestrated, choreographed, costumed, so-phisticated concerts, knowing that she is born the same year as me, not Brittney Spears. I keep my public persona as energetic, youthful, talent-ed, and real as she does. She's a Leo. I'm a Taurus. We probably would not get along. I wonder what she would think if she got the chance to read this.

If I could have rescued Michael Jackson to provide respite from his frenemies in my humble home, and gotten him to just drop the charade of being a character for the world and just be happy and gay, I would have secured him in secret to assist him in becoming real about himself, and maybe saved his life. Then there's Prince. I am addicted to pres-criptive meds myself, Xanax, and I resent the medical community for the stabs at undoing the damage I did to myself by partying on illicit drugs for 25 years. Prescribing a legal but lethal medication for my acute anxiety is a catch-22, and the subject of my second book: *DRxug of Choice: Pick your Poison*. That Prince was behind the wheel of one of his automobiles to visit a local chain of pharmacies to fulfill the ever-increasing quota of narcotics his drug addled body required demonstrates the insidiousness of his substance abuse overshadowing his talent and celebrity. He had a number of prescriptions valid at a number of nationally known pharmacies that ensured his addiction always had a backup. And he was so desperate he drove himself to a pharmacy not even incognito. Where were his personal assistants???

Now, it's just Madge and me. And I can dance as good as her Alvin Ailey white ass can. We both learned from veterans of early R&B who introduced us to the then underground world of disco in the 1970's.

Note to Madonna: I liked *Confessions on a Dance Floor* as it was the best album produced since *Erotica*. It was relatable to me. I was a burlesque dancer, I love the baseline disco beat of the songs, and I appreciate the old-school mixing of one song into the next like in the underground disco's where the DJ could really mix one song over and over and over. Madonna: Try reading my confessional book of being a hoofer: *Homo GoGo Man, A Fairytale About A Boy Who Grew Up In Discoland* by Christopher Duquette.

P.S.: My 60th birthday was a disappointment. Revisiting Fire Island after a long hiatus reminded me that places as well as people change. Fire Island today is not how I left it 12 years ago. And memories are a fairytale when youth and beauty were worth more than money for an overpriced trip to the past. Fire Island looked sad and lonely. I will embrace the memories of good times. I've learned to minimize my lifestyle, and I am so grateful for what little I have and what little I need in life.

CHAPTER 4

PO'TOWN HOES

Bravo presents the Po'town Hoes of Main Street, Poughkeepsie
Apres le Hairdresser's Disco Ball of Hudson Valley

FOR THE LAST FOUR YEARS, HUDSON VALLEY has hosted a non-profit event, the Hairdresser's Disco Ball, wherein local Hairdresser Salons produce an over-the-top celebration of hair and makeup to reflect a theme agreed upon each year as a campy runway show to raise money to support the treatment of those inflicted and suffering from AIDS.

The theme of the 2015 show was *Hair of the Future.* I was a participant in the show, wearing nothing but a speedo spray painted gold to interact pre-show with the guests.

Kylie J. Winn has always been the popular host of the show. He is a renowned haircutter, hairstylist, and make-up artist, as well a celebrity wherever he goes, daytime, nighttime, in straight venues as well as gay. Kylie stands over 6 feet tall. But when he puts on heels and a headdress, he becomes a mammoth proud manifestation of fur and hair and mascara as intimidating as Grace Jones. While hosting the Disco Ball, he can whip the microphone around like a jostling bar to keep human's away from his "Grace in your Face" attitude and presence. He commands your attention. Kylie works on his natural high energy and some J&B. The Hairdresser's Disco Ball is a success every year because Kylie J. Winn knows how to turn out a fierce Vogue Ball.

Once Kylie starts turning up the volume of another alter-egos, Tina Turner, there is no stopping the range of his charm and popularity in

Po'town, where he lives, on Main Street, in a second floor loft that looks over the Main Drag like a bordello with live prostitutes in the window 24/7 like in Amsterdam. Big glass panes of floor to ceiling windows allow Kylie and his menagerie of party boys/girls who are always in company to blow kisses to the passing audience, and those pedestrians passing the window to this circus will look up to see a full size fun house of flesh on display.

I showed up at Kylie's trailer of trash apartment on a Monday afternoon, the day after the ball, to find three larger than life drag queens perfecting their poisonous looks. Kylie had gone from the solo artist, Tina Turner, to chief of the band, Patti LaBelle, with her backup girls Devon, a beautiful Puerto Rican boy who was rocking a Joan Jett look, and Biscuit, a perfectly proportioned black man with unnaturally blue eyes and a perpetual erection. Between the high heels on their boots and pumps, short skirts barely baring their true genders but extenuating their muscular legs, large oversized fake fur caps puffing their upper torsos into the size of linebackers, messy wigs reflecting the fact that Monday is the hairdresser's day off, weekend beards that are now in their third day of overgrowth, and the lack of makeup and jewelry gave the trio a prehistoric look: Mammoth Mammals.

The three shaggy ladies of the afternoon had been "YouTube-ing" their alter-egos while in drag and sprawling onto large vacant vehicles parked on Main Street, Po'town. The Mammoth 'Girls' have been letting the world know that they are more interesting than any Bravo 'Housewives of X' project that had been entertaining America sitting on their couches wearing their Snuggies.

What these girls wanted and desired made 'Housewives of New Jersey' look like ashes from a cigarette. Kylie and his reinforcements are hotter than volcanoes coming out of Hawaii. What they had to say, still highly lubricated from the Hairdresser's Disco Ball is exclusive to You Tube.

CHAPTER 5

ESCAPE FROM NYC:

A Middle-Aged Gay Man's Lost Summer in Greece. A Modern-Day Version of a Tennessee Williams Drama.

I AM LIVING ON THE EDGE of a very thin dime. I've paid my exorbitant rent for a substandard raw loft space in the newly discovered lawless bohemia of Williamsburg, Brooklyn, on time for 3 years, changed the décor to incite my location production business, rented my rare vintage 1973 Volvo 1800ES Sportwagon, and even offered my iconic vintage ward-robe for work in an industry that even after my charm and flexibility, could not make my well promoted production company, BurgShoot, Inc, profitable. FDR, the 32nd President of the United States, who shares his initials with my bank rich uncle in New Hampshire, Francis D. Roy, provides the presidential profile to the only cash asset I have at this point: 10 cents. I have squeezed all available cash advances from six once bountiful credit cards to make my rent in the most elusive and exclusive loft building in this pioneer land: Williamsburg, Brooklyn. There is no way that I can stay one more month, after 3 years of living like some kind of trust fund child of FDR, in an old doll factory turned into a boarding house for wayward bohemians. I am the oldest and probably the most unemployable in residence, with my daily drug and alcohol consumption. My hopes and dreams of distributing unique business cards made from wood panel samples I would stuff in my pockets from the Home Depot cabinet department were unique, containing my contact information, but did not produce profitable results. I was in the red. Fire Engine Red.

151 Kent Avenue is a three-story red brick building on the Brooklyn waterfront that was cut up into both large and very small loft apartments for rent as advertised in the Village Voice: RAW LVG LOFT SPACES $1500 & UP. I acquired the smallest space, 800 square feet, sixty feet long, 20-foot-high unfinished ceilings, foot-wide wood plank floors embedded with tar and the remains of doll parts, and a single ten-foot-high window looking out over a very active recycle center, the East River, and the entire skyline from Northern Manhattan to the South, pre-9/11.

I lived with Italian made knock-offs of renown architectural furniture mixed with the real deal, fur rugs and throws, borrowed and gifted artwork (read: sentimental value to those that gave them to me) hanging on the gallery-white long unobstructed walls, as well as relics from the street and coastal castaways I discovered as I traveled through the streets of Brooklyn, Manhattan, and Queens. It's both a pirates discovery of treasure and dumpster diving to spot and quickly deposit a roadside acquisition with no history that your nighttime fantasy mind sees as Tiffany quality when it turns out to be Canal Street junk.

But the day of reckoning was apparent when I realized I would not be able to make rent for the first time in my life. I sold as much of my possessions as I could, as well as all my Century 21 designer duds liquidated now at the new bohemian Williamsburg flea markets and consignment shops while living on my last month's rent. When I first moved to NYC, I had made an oath that my monthly rent was the most foremost priority of my wages. I could be short on milk or new wardrobe, but I would never want to encounter an eviction notice in the space that I could at least provide me with sanctity from my hectic lifestyle. Sleep, hibernating from a binge, and ignoring uninvited solicitors knocking at my door.

But the writing was on the wall. I had depleted the last of my credit card advances, and knew that I would not be able to make the next month's rent, regardless of my security held by the landlord who was not negotiable about using that asset as covering the last month's rent. I was more concerned with personally performing the handyman jobs necessary to return the loft to the landlord in the same if not better condition than when I first rented it. There was no formal walk through, but I was assured by the rental agent for the 'Doll House' that the loft showed well, and the landlord was going to be in a windfall. It was undisputed that I deserved my security in full. The question was when?

I was moving out without a tangible plan. I bought two yellow plastic Samsonite suitcases, an Apple laptop and a one-way ticket to Athens, Greece. And all the crystal meth I could buy with $1000 in cash to spare.

I had no more credit on my plastic cards. They were all in default. The only form of large credit charge I possessed was an American Express Business Card, which I paid in full each month as is their policy.

My grand plan was to arrive pre-summer before the 2004 Olympics in Athens to find work with my skills as an English-speaking go-getter. No contacts. No leads. Just my crystal-induced charm and two yellow suitcases of designer clothes from sample sales and employee discounts in NYC.

My ex said I was behaving suicidal. He died 9 months after making that statement to me after he failed at a suicide attempt followed 2 weeks later by one successful drug overdose. Be careful of the final words a loved one may say, as you can't really see yourself accurately in the mirror of life. As ugly a breakup could be, your ex will give you more honest truths as hurtful as the words may sound. He sincerely and carefully said that he saw the I was demonstrating actions that could be interpreted as suicidal at the time: selling off all of my marketable possessions (art and furniture), surrendering a pile of high-end well maintained designer clothes to consignment shops, and giving a lot of my excess wardrobe to friends I knew would like and benefit from them. No one rejected my offerings, and I meant well. 15 months after my ex passed away, I was still blind to see my own serious attempt at ending my life as a projection of my ex's unobjective opinion about what was probably not difficult to calculate given the facts. I was deaf, dumb, and blind, like the 'Who's' operatic 'Tommy.'

The day before my departure to Greece, my sister's girlfriend, a lawyer with the reputation of a bulldog, called on the phone of my neighbor's loft that I was hiding out in until my exile. How she got this phone number I don't know. Perhaps an emergency number I had given my parents? I never underestimated the power of my seriously moral and ethically legal sister-in-law. Sometimes she had my back; other times I had to beware of her with her relationship to the law, an institution I seemed to always see as an adversity to my progressive take on life in the fast lane.

I had absconded $10,000 from an equity loan I still had access to after signing over the ownership of a beautifully restored architecturally unique house in the quant Arlington Park area of downtown Buffalo. My sister's girlfriend had been buying me out of the investment that I had put into the property purchase and upgrade of the high mainten-ance historic house for the past three years, which fed my slacker druggy faux entrepreneur live-style in Williamsburg, NYC. When the checks stopped coming, there was no real work of substance to pay the rent, the credit cards were dry, and I only had a collection of FDR dimes. Then like a guardian angel was available to help me, I discovered that I has access to an equity loan on the Arlington Park house I had invested a substantial down payment on, that provided me with an amusement park top prize of $10,000 I could dispense from the Citibank ATM as easy and anonymously as an account inquiry. I wasn't coherent to pro-ject the ramifications of this underserved pot of gold. I was a drug addict provided with a financial extension on my irresponsible lifestyle.

My sister's girlfriend had discovered the lien, my jackpot $10,000. on the house I bought, and she was about to sell. She and my shocked sister were about to lose a deal on the closing of the house now that they knew that $10,000 was owed to Citibank before the house could be sold. My sister's girlfriend was irate, threatening to send police offi-cers to all the international airports to prevent me from escaping from NYC. I told my sobbing sister on an extension phone to take her head out of the sand if she was to go on living with her profit-hungry lover, as if I was entitled to take the $10,000 in question. I was a drug addict who was not going to turn myself in without a good fight built on a fairy tale defense.

I bolted from my neighbor's apartment as if I was truly threatened by my bull-dog lawyer sister-in-law's threats of legal action before hiring a car service for Newark Airport as Air Lingus took me and my two duck yellow suitcases to Berlin, then boarded Air Greece to Athens, with no other destination in mind but a location I was familiar with from an add-ictive vacation to the most gay-friendly Greek Island, Mykonos, where

I had found grassroots accommodations twenty years earlier on a discounted holiday with my then flight attendant lover Fernando.

I arrived in Athens in not exactly in one piece; I was minus one large duck yellow Samsonite suitcase that went incomprehensibly missing from Berlin to Athens, separated from its Siamese twin yellow suitcase that arrived alone in Athens International Airport. Where and how a baggage handler could separate two so obviously identical suitcases from one flight is beyond intercontinental comprehension. All I cared about was that the yellow Samsonite suitcase I did successfully claim from the baggage go-round in Athens contained my bounty of crystal meth that I was my own mule for illegally importing to Greece for my own personal use and existence. After the Air Lingus Baggage Agent presented me with an airline baggage brochure to help identify my very outrageously example of missing luggage that was a maternal twin to the one in my possession, I put her customer service training to task, that it was not your standard luggage that their Missing Luggage standard form would help more than presenting an example of the duck yellow Samsonite I had in my possession to model. I was tired and had a hotel reservation I wanted to retire to: the Four Seasons hotel, where I thought that by providing my next high-end domicile, would incite some level of respect to Herr Baggage Handler, but she was not amused. Where in the universe my twin plastic yellow storage pod had traveled to, it was to be reunited with its identical twin at the Four Seasons Hotel, in Athens, Greece. Incredible that these two outrageously unique suitcases could ever have been separated by any human that is not color blind, I was enjoying my opportunity to be outrageously arrogant to a representative of an airline that could not offer solace or a possible explanation to this debacle. But my trump card was giving the 'Four Seasons' Hotel as where they should air shuttle my suitcase as someone I was good at portraying: an entitled unsatisfied customer who was not going to be as angry as I felt I was entitled to be. Again: I am only playing the character of a fictitious drama. I just knew I was on my own, and without any colleagues to calm my hysteria, I played the part of the disgruntled trust fund child spoiled by deserving the best things in life. Find my damn duck yellow Samsonite luggage and deliver it 1st class to my 1st class accommodations at the 'Four Seasons' Hotel. Sometimes it is necessary and esteem building to have a public hissy fit. Amends can always be made later.

I was confident the scalawag suitcase would meet up with me and its twin companion traveler at the Intercontinental Four Seasons Hotel as I left the air-conditioned Athens's airport to encounter the combination of arid and humid atmosphere of ancient Greece. The gypsy cab was not air-conditioned as it took me on the ancient road from the airport to the more contemporary superhighways of busy Athens and finally as close to the Four Seasons hotel as I the cab could take me. The entire block surrounding the International Hotel was barricaded from automobile traffic with local cops and United Nation's security teams outfitted with semi-automatic weapons not to keep me, but any terrorists, from coming close to the Hotel and its current guests consist-ing of dignitaries from around the world to participate in a summit on the first anniversary of the September 11, 2001, to propose prevention of any-more horrific terrorist hi-jacks and attacks on iconic international build-ings, or any other targets of prominence in the world.

I had no precedent knowledge of this when I chose the Four Seasons as my first landing spot on my escape from NYC on September 11, 2002. I did not even have reservations in this most prominent Inn with the possibility of no vacancies due to the forecasted summit to such a monumental event on the very day of its anniversary, forever referred to as 9/11. I had to wheel my singular canary yellow Samsonite under the barricade to have my passport cleared by a UN guard, and eye-balled by the rest of the security and cops as I wheeled my way into the only familiar tony address, I felt comfortable to seek refuse in on this danger-ously unscripted storyline of my escape from NYC.

I checked into a standard room at the rate of $450.00. I did not even take advantage of internet hotel discount sites before committing to this ridiculously over-priced hotel room I approved of and did not dispute even after being informed that the pool that I had sunned and swum in twenty years ago, immortalized in a zebra print brief swimming trunk photographed by my lover Fernando as I runway walked along the edge of the pool with the 70's modern distorted mirror wall that reflected my chiseled physique. It was currently closed for renovations. Besides the complimentary breakfast and the gym and the internet access, the pool was one of the necessary amenities I was counting on in the $450.00 daily fee I was paying to stay at the Four Seasons. At least my errant Samsonite luggage and Air Lingus Baggage agent would be impressed when it was finally recovered and delivered to the swanky, out of my budget, hotel address. I was flying solo, so I had to stand by my executive decision to get into a hotel room that I was familiar but not in my budget just to avoid a nervous breakdown from my irresponsible decisions not to mention my lifestyle.

There were gentlemen sporting conservative business suits and ethnic formal attire from all races and cultures, very few if no women, loitering in the hotel lobby with its 100 foot ceilings and mezzanines from all 5 floors of luxury hotel rooms with hanging topiary, gurgling indoor water friezes, and me with my East Village casual blue jeans, black lumber jack boots, and white V-neck T-shirt walking behind a formally costumed Greek bellhop parading the only spot of yellow in the room, my sole suitcase, on a brass baggage carrier to the elevators that would take us to the fifth floor executive wing smoking room 523 I had been booked into, overlooking the outdoor pool currently under construction. I tipped the bellhop, asked where I could purchase a bottle of vodka close by, and locked the door to retrieve my carefully concealed eighth of an ounce of crystal meth to ensure its safe passage and partake in a sample. Chemically medicated, I replant my illegal substance in my suitcase while I stepped out of the hotel and navigated under the police barricades to journey into the alien neighborhood to procure vodka.

I found a small grocery store that sold produce, cold cuts, ice cream confections, cigarettes, and a local vodka at a price that I think was high roughly translated into dollars. I had to pay in cash as I found that the only credit card I was could rely on was my American Express business card for BurgShoot, Inc., the lucrative production company I created and kept alive with small amounts of income renting everything from my loft, the rooftop, my furniture, clothes, and my vintage orange Volvo 1800ES Sportwagon for movie, TV, and photo shoots. I did not think that Greece, and most of the rest of the world, would no longer embrace American Express, as they did not embrace America, ironically on the anniversary of the tragedy of 9/11, with the same deferent privilege.

America had lost its panache. Overseas merchants preferred Visa or Mastercard, or cash, which I ended up using on my first purchase abroad on the vodka, and consequentially on all other transactions with the exception of hotels, who accepted the American Express card as reliable currency.

I scurried back to the safety and security of the barricaded Four Seasons, rushed to my fifth floor room like an addict with his fix in hand to the Executive Wing to get tweaked on vodka, crystal, cigarettes, and internet porn from the master of homoerotic images, Kristen Bjorn. I trimmed my body hair in the marble bathroom fit for a star, and took the first images of my nude torso with my digital camera, downloaded onto my laptop to tweak in photoshop, with images that I would use to secure future dance and escort bookings on the internet over the next 3 years. My $450.00 Four Seasons Hotel room was my first debt I would start amounting to securing paying for my drug and alcohol lifestyle in Greece.

The only interruption I experienced was the bellhop delivering my erstwhile yellow Samsonite about eight hours after check-in. I did not act emotionally ecstatic but more nonchalant like this had been an inconvenient experience. Again, playing the part of an entitled subject in a well-played role. I did not visit the pool in construction, the gym, nor the dining area, but did venture out of the hotel at 10:00pm to find 'whatever': a gay bar, a dance club, a cheap easy bite to eat, or some companionship, male, Greek, and not for hire. I was hungry, lonely, horny but far from tired.

As soon as I left the confines of the Four Season's Hotel, I passed a large gentleman's club down the street, with suggestive female strippers overtly hanging out at the entrance with the busty bouncers to get some business. I got more sexually excited, but stayed away from this venue as if my homosexuality would send feisty guard dogs to attach their deadly teeth to my ankles to distribute the pain of my depression of being alone from my soul to my body, with no emergency contact, no language skills, and drugs and cash in my possession. I have always believed my innate karma has protected me from any assault to my person or home. I knew enough to stay clear of the strip club, as exciting it seemed to my tired and lonesome condition.

I trekked around nocturnal Athens aimlessly with no sense of direction until I realized the whole city is built around the sacred historically protected grounds of the Prometheus, atop the hill overlooking all of the sprawling urban city that hosted the very first and the next Olympic Athletic competition. I followed residential roads that bordered the cap of the city that contained more ancient artifacts of civilization after Byzantine Egypt. The road that I followed, hoping to find a Disco, Gay Bar, or stranger-friendly cafe, is the perimeter of the ancient hallowed grounds that are protected from private development by nothing more than a stone wall. I could jump the wall to trespass on the park area full of trees and roads and buildings, official and ancient, but I stayed out of the shadowy area for fear of being jumped by a teenager or attacked by a wild animal or encounter a shady character like myself. I was in an unknown territory, alone.

I accidently discovered a dance club that was boarded up. By reading the club posters I came realize that this club, and all other nocturnal activities like clubbing in Athens, Greece are seasonal. The clubs in Athens close in the summer as the young blood work and play on the Greek islands until they return at the end of the Greek summer, October. I am thirsty, my feet encased in logger boots are tired. I'm not exactly hungry as I am still tweaking from crystal, and I am worried about how to navigate back to my hotel.

Eventually I find the superhighway that transported me to the hotel earlier the day before (it is well after midnight now) and migrate along the busy road, too fearful to hail a cab to hasten the trip as I am too high and can't move my jowls to talk. I have lock jaw. I need more vodka that is waiting in my Executive room. As I pass the strip club near the Four Seasons Hotel, I imagine how horny the gentlemen in the stripper club might be, like me. I have never been interested in sex with a heterosexual man as I like to be sexually reciprocated or adored like the exhustler who was used to being objectified on a pedestal.

I am back in my room. I nourish myself with the clear alcohol mixed with cranberry juice, find out from the front desk the earliest ferry to Mykonos, and stay up all night in my room full of vices (internet porn) until I visit the breakfast nook on my floor for some eggs, bacon and strong coffee surrounded by businessmen in conservative suits already interacting with their professional partners over espresso and croissants. Nobody seems to pay me any mind. I tip and leave the breakfast area fueled for the morning of checking out, entering a cab waiting at the hotel entrance for a taxi to take me to the shipping district, busy in the morning with cargo to disperse large ferries to carry humans, local Greeks, on their way to work or families abroad, as well as a few travelers like myself who did not have the wherewithal to book an air flight from Athens to the Greek islands. I am only repeating the method that was previously used by my flight attendant boyfriend twenty years ago to get to the Gay Mecca Mykonos; the slow and local ferry.

The ferry is half full of adventurous travelers who are willing to stow their luggage themselves and locate an unreserved seat or dining booth by the window for the eight-hour local ferry to the island of horny satyrs. The flight from Athens to Mykonos by a commercial, island-hopping airlines is five times the price of the $45.00 ferry faire, but only a half-hour in precious holiday time. Because they do not take American Express on either system of transport, I must pay what little cash I carried with me after buying my Apple Laptop and two yellow Samsonite suitcases before escaping NYC. I bundled some buns with butter from my Four Seasons breakfast buffet to save me from buying concessions on board the ferry. I bite into one, crack a molar on my lower bridge of my otherwise perfectly maintained teeth, and suffer the rest of my stay in Greece with the rough pointy remains of the broken tooth, and the sensitivity to the exposed area, which I learn to get use to like all other hardships I learn to cope with while drug addicted, destitute, helpless, and far from home. It all falls on my shoulders.

The ferry arrives in the familiar port of the island of Mykonos, the white stucco village still quant even though there has been a lot of commercial development around the ancient tightly packed village with large hotels to accommodate the high increase in tourism. Twenty years ago when I first visited the island with my first lover, we secured very rustic accommodations from a local landlord waiting for ambitious young travelers like us to pay for a two story apartment with a funky kitchen and bath above a liquor store with a veranda overlooking the foot traffic on the narrow sidewalks below. We paid $50 cash per week and ended up staying three weeks. The liquor store's proximity got me addicted to the crimson Campari liquor; that I would drink a liter daily with OJ, vodka, or straight up. The wealthier visitors had yachts moored in the then tiny port and taxied to villas far from the cacophony of the busy town. These visitors were known as jetsetters, as Mykonos was hardly the sole destination for them on their voyage, or all of the other international trips their lifestyles could afford in one working year.

This time, I take a crowded bus that travels along the ledge of a one lane road carved into the orange landscape that follows the ocean. The path the bus takes is the first layer of the exquisite island's perimeter. There are the burnt remains of two commercial vehicles lying in the sandy beach that presumably fell off the dangerous road that transports both suicidal and presumably normal visitors to the island of Mykonos; I am the former. One is a cargo transporter on its side with the four large rubber tires intact as it rests on its driver's side, the cargo it was carrying when it lost it's footing on the road above is missing. It could have been a stack of plastic chairs for the outdoor cafes, or it could have been a parcel of fresh cut flowers to fill the Hellenic vases in the hotels and restaurants when it spilled down the ravine to the island's shore to be washed out to sea. The other vehicle I see is a bus, similar to the one I am standing in, on its back, the roof crumbled and sparkling blue glass framing the dead vehicle that slipped off the ledge above, with or without a full load of passengers' DNA woven into the tapestry of the accidental art work. I ponder the possible prophecy of the bus I am riding in, and with my devil may care suicidal attitude toward my life, and laissez-faire attitude about everyone else's in the world, like on my intercontinental flight from NYC. I think of the perks of dying in the burning metal and glass carnage of the bus I am standing and alive in slipping from the ledge of the perilous roadway and landing next on the beach close to the existing accidental bus traveling into a holiday in Mykonos. I would not have to be seen dragging my plastic duck valises on wheels over the cobble stone promenade and sidewalks looking for accommodations that with my only means of payment, my American Express Business Card. It seems like a viable ending to my story.

I end up getting a ride on the back of a tripod motorcycle with a storage wagon to carry my two ugly duckling suitcases from a friendly Greek man. All Greek men on the island of Mykonos, young, old, handsome, homely, local or working the long summer away from their wives, girlfriends, and families in Athens are flirtatiously friendly with men, especially American, and women, especially young and attractive, while working their jobs or on their own time. I experience this more intensely on this trip than my last, as I am not encumbered by a lover, and I am under the influence of a drug that has highly sexual powers that affect the user as well as those in their immediate vicinity. That's why crystal meth is so popular with gay men; it empowers them with sexual confidence that supersedes any insecurity and paranoia most gay men suffer from.

My tripod driver suggests a sprawling gay hotel that he assures me will take my plastic credit card. The hotel is one of the more beautifully appointed resorts situated at the very summit of the coastal village, providing a sweeping view of all of the town below including the famous ancient windmill, the port full of fishing, private yachts, ferries, commercial liners, and the Mediterranean Ocean and other Greek Islands beyond. I will have to walk the tremendously steeps stairs and roadways to get down to the busy town for food, alcohol, and nightlife, but at least I was spared the hassle of dragging my heavily packed suitcases up to a hotel entrance myself. I tip my ride handsomely for identifying a more than aesthetically satisfactory hotel, reducing what limited cash I have for transporting me to a picturesque hotel that I had no knowledge of, and am assured by my caring driver that I will probably see him around the gay hotel over my stay, initially planned as a two week stay.

Like every other structure on the island of Mykonos, the Elysium Hotel is stark white, tiered along the step peek of the hillside with various connected and independent buildings housing a variety of layouts of living accommodations for the primarily male gay guests. I step up to the dark mahogany dining table that serves as a front desk while guests are engrossed in reading international daily newspapers in the adjoining lobby, and others are lunching and lurching in the mezzanine dining area. Most all eyes are on me and my yellow traveling companions. I secure a balcony room on the second floor, the best view in the hotel, and am relieved that there is what the front desk man describes as a full gym on the premises. I need to work out as much as I need to take crystal meth.

My room is more than satisfactory, as most travelers find that the lack of a bath in lieu of a small, tiled corner with a shower wand to remove debris from the body while squatting is the standard of showering outside of bathtub / shower obsessed Americans. And yet we don't seem to recognize the amenity of a bidet! My room is at the end of the two story white structure that contains twenty of the same white pillow-comfy rooms with doors facing the east morning sun, the balcony on the top floor and patio on the lower floor facing the guaranteed orange sunsets over the Mediterranean Ocean every evening. This is where the story telling turns from sounding like a travel brochure and into a wasteful experience of a hopeless drug addict.

Crystal is procured from my black nylon shoulder bag with a only a small white radioactive symbol identifying itself as part of the subtle Helmet Lang collection, that perfectly holds my artic white Apple laptop that is preserved in a Gianni Versace black cotton bag to prevent designer urchins from contaminating my drive that is full of pictures of Greece, some Word journaling, and reams of Kristen Bjorn all-male porn stills from his movies, with a lot of Mediterranean erections lit to photographic perfection. I do a bump, unpack, and go to the gym room which has two dangerous panes of sliding glass doors making any activity in the weight room visible to outside spectators, in addition to wall length and mirror. I could bleed to death with one five-pound dumbbell plummeting all of these glass surfaces. I can't stop the suicidal thoughts. I do not think I am ever going to return to the States. I am internationally homeless.

I work out as heavy as I can in spite of the strange and limited equipment. I have opened the sliding glass door and all of the windows in this freestanding structure for air to circulate. I have stripped my tank top off as there is nobody or a printed policy stating I can't, which draws the attention of some of hotel guests whose rooms are located on the same grounds as the gym and the hotel laundry room. I overhear a sixty-something bald man tells his younger companion that he might want to get in shape while he is staying at the Elysée Hotel. His ground-floor room has a sliding glass pane that faces the gym and is curtained to prevent me from understanding the dynamics of their relationship. I'm getting sweaty and pumped up with the basic equipment that only provides a fraction of the intensity of a workout I am used to in my familiar hard-core gym back in NYC. But this is not America, where gyms are as important as medical facilities. The quality of the gyms I have visited abroad are reflective of the physique of the indigenous population; from lean muscle to completely out of shape.

Before long I am not the only one in this gym of steel weights and glass walls; another guest has come to join me. He is not American judging by his gym-wear (skinny tank and short shorts), and he is more unfamiliar with the alien equipment than I was when I first took in the inventory when I started my work out over an hour ago. I nod hello, but do not engage in any small talk with the other gym body because I don't see us having sex together. I am horny on crystal, but, in situations where I am not desperate, like when I am enjoying a workout or an inspirational song is broadcast on the disco dance floor, I can be very picky. I leave the gym after two hours of working out, and head straight for the poolside bar where I can order some fast protein in the form of a double quarter-pound hamburger with blue cheese, no fries, and a White Russian for a protein and caffeine post-workout meal.

I've got my Helmet Lang man's shoulder bag with me, with my laptop, Gucci sunglasses, and Gucci brown bikini stored in the bag. So after I charge the meal to my room bill that is so far being approved by American Express, I change in the poolside men's room into my swimwear and without hesitation dive into the pool surrounded by gay vacationers from around the world who are curious as to who the new solo body is that swims so athletically from one end of the pool to the other. I was blessed with early swim lessons from summer camp, which I advanced from Red Cross Lifeguard to Water Safety Instructor to find summer employment that empowered me, physically and emotionally. The brown Gucci bikini is cut perfectly with heavy material that dries out fast, but when the suit gets wet, it is hell trying to keep it on my hips. Love Tom Ford's aesthetics but would offer constructive reviews on his Gucci men's wardrobe, all courtesy of my last lover employed at the flagship Fifth Avenue store at a considerable discount as most were returned items, disqualifying them from being presented in the invent-tory of unworn merchandise. Does 90% off the retail price sound easy for a generous boyfriend who took pride in my appearance sound ridiculous?

When I dive into a body of water, the Gucci suit sucks up enough water to turn the sexy brown bikini into a sponge that rests below my ass cheeks until I swiftly pull the waterlogged swimsuit above my hips so I can climb out of the pool without exposing my 42 year old derrière. I find an iron-wrought table and chair under a veranda that will filter some of the Mediterranean sun from my unprotected fair skin so I can write and take pictures that I can download to my laptop and Photoshop. It's like digital needlecraft. This will be my daily afternoon regime as long as I stay in the Elyesse Hotel for the next 4 weeks. Gym, Bluecheese burgers, shower and change in the poolside men's room, a swim in the pool, and work on my laptop. I order White Russians, switch to Black Russians, and finally Cosmopolitans at sunset.

I don't make friends easily. I seem to put off the rest of the guests with my body, wardrobe, ability to dive and swim perfectly, and my intense relationship with my laptop. I don't see anyone I want to meet to have sex with, except a large, well-built Greek man who seems to know the staff, sunbathes almost every day in a speedo, and sometimes takes the speedo off when he is tanning his backside. I don't know his name. I don't ask the bartender or waiters what his name is or anything about him. I can see he is uncut, so he is not American. He doesn't make any overtures towards me, so I ignore him, for four weeks. Homosexual courtships have always been based on natural introductions, which can take forever, or never.

The first night I arrive in the Elysée hotel, I can't sleep, even though I think I should. I lie in bed and watch Greek television that I do not understand. Around 2am I hear electronic disco music emanating from the heart of the village below. I try to discern where it is coming from. I don't know where the discos are after my last visit twenty years ago. By 4am, I endow my courage to go out to investigate, weary that I do not have the funds to pay for a door charge, must less bar drinks. I have only about $200.00 American dollars that I need to budget for whatever expense does not accept my American Express, like the ferry back to Athens, transportation to the airport to leave Greece, transport back to

NYC upon arriving in Newark. I'm living on two dimes. Each worth $100.00.

After taking a bump of crystal, I play some old-school disco I downloaded to my laptop, Donna Summer "Once Upon a Time" opera of a women going mad. The track "Faster and Faster to Nowhere" is spinning me into my NYC nightlife wardrobe to make my entrance to after-hours Mykonos society on this "Fairy Tale High" that Tina (gay reference to Meth) has been staging my life the last 3 years. I put on my standard attention getting outfit that I wear when I am going someplace new, but have worn hundreds of times: an off-white Costume National long sleeve pull-over body hugging shirt with a zipper and collar for formal occasions, Helmet Lang boot-leg jeans frayed at every detailed edge, and Larry Mahan gold snake-skin cowboy boots from El Paso, Texas. This is a uniform I would wear for a nightlife society interview. It fits me well, and I wear it well. As Donna Summer is jamming to "Working the Midnight Shift," I give my buzzed and choppy hair some product to make it spike around the entire crown of my hair, and leave my room to find where the action is on this island of sin at this hour of the night turning into morning.

The cowboy boots were not the best choice for scaling down the steps from the hotel to the town, and I slip a step and slide down the smoothed stone staircase but catch my bearings at the bottom to resume my cowboy slag dragging my heels as I make enough clomping on the stone walk to sound like a shoed horse. I never find the disco where the music was emanating from, probably because they have closed, as I see drunken revelers hanging onto each other searching for the port side cafes. Nobody notices me; I am invisible. I was not in the same disco drama that these players participated in, so I do not exist to them. I feel very overdressed, conspicuous, and lonely. I had planned to catch the cusp of the night and with my getup and good looks, I thought I would make some after-hours friends to go to another club, party, bar, yacht, hotel room, to hear more music, do more drugs, drink more drinks, and hopefully converse with someone in English.

Driven by some sixth sense, I shuffle in my cowboy boots to the peninsula of rocks that the Mediterranean Ocean slaps against, and gay men troll around for last call sex. My cowboy boots are more impossible to navigate the wet coastal rocks, and I feel even more ridiculous as I struggle to keep from falling into the ocean and try to stay dry, as men in more practical gear watch and follow me. I always want to stride with grace. I stop when I see two young men fornicating like seals on the breakers. White water is cascading over the barrier rock as one Mediterranean man is sexually drilling into the back of a younger Mediterranean man. I think I hear howls of nature echoing off the wet rocks. I am not aroused but overwhelmed by witnessing this primal mating that seems to be indigenous to the island of Mykonos. I am satisfied with my nocturnal hunt and retire to my room with my cowboy boots chafing my feet. A film scene I had done my best to satisfy the producers but would inevitably be cut by the editors as not relevant or good enough for the fantastic fairytale perception of my pretentious life.

The next night I decide to go out earlier and locate the source of the music and frivolity. I dress more sensibly, in black leather logger boots, cuffed jeans, and a Black V-neck T-shirt that would work in the East Village and Upper East Side of NYC, Berlin, and Mykonos at night. Tom of Finland chic. Two attached two-story clubs are sharing the same crowd that are dancing on the DJ'd dance floor, no charge, so I enter unobserved, climb up a set of stairs to a rooftop bar with pre-taped music, which overlooks the balcony of the adjoining joint, where more revelers are holding their pastel drinks high in the air. I climb down to another half empty, cheaply lit dance floor. I follow what resembles a hamster trail twice threading through the two attached discos, get frustrated and to tired. The common area is the courtyard sprinkled with arrant tables and fallen chairs with the white steps of Mykonos Town Hall to the right. I encounter from one serendipity from the very place I am trying to escape: NYC. His name is Albin. I know him from an upper East Side hairdresser circuit that meets for dinner parties in my old party friend Marco's.

It is a relief to finally find someone who can validate my existence on the other side of the earth. There is no sexual chemistry between us, but Albin is happy to see me as he knows I like to party. Albin is travelling through the Greek islands with his staid friend Cyrus, who happens to be Iranian, like my lover who I am running away from, Shary. Only Cyrus is not hooked on crystal meth. Like Shary, he is educated, well-mannered, and gay. Unlike Shary, he is tall, and not as interested in body building and grooming himself to be a peacock. Cyrus is a serious intellectual. He is here with Albin to take in the historical sites as well as the pleasure beaches and nightlife. I am so happy to have their company for the few days while they are staying in a modest apartment timeshare comparable to the flat I stayed in 20 years ago when I first visited Mykonos, which at that time did not have the deluxe hotels high above the town developed yet. We made a bond to stick together for the limited days they were staying in Mykonos, where I never set a bookend to my stay, as I was a nomad with no place to call home.

I leave Albin, Cyrus, and the discos on our introductory night to walk back to my hilltop hotel by way of the bay, where I have seen couples fornicating in the daytime. The moon is lighting the stage of the bay, the pier, and the surrounding village. I am horny, and hot, and decide to skinny dip. I take my clothes off with no one around, prance to the end of the pier, dive in and swim a few strokes into the dark bay. A motorcycle comes to a stop at street level. The rider takes his helmet off, shakes his hair, looks down into the bay making it clear that I am the object of his attention, stores his helmet, and walks down the sandy steps to the beach that precedes the pier. I can't believe this is happening. I don't know if this guy is going to innocently join me in a late-night swim, or if he is just going to watch me. He leans against the stone wall that holds the port from the bay, with shiny leggings, either nylon or leather, one propped up, like a cowboy would. I swim back to the pier so I can step up the ladder to walk naked in the moonlight back to my clothes, where I re-dress quickly. I'm not sure if this biker is taking a sober break from his alcohol fueled night, or if he is looking for some sexual action, male or female, down by the bay. I am not nervous, but I do want to make the right signals to connect with this biker. I can see that he is lean, and dressed in nylon bike wear, but I can't make out his face.

With my boots in my hand, I walk towards the sandy stairs, but make a detour towards the stone wall that the biker is posing on, lean next to him to say "nice night" in English, and he returns by attaching himself to my lips for the longest open mouth kiss I have experienced since my ex-lover, Shary, met me 10 years ago. We kiss and grope each other under the moonlight with no audience until I suggest my hotel room as the next stage for our Greek man-on-man affair.

In the streetlights, I can see that he is very handsome, my height, Greek, locks of curly hair, knowledgeable of my hotel, and bi-sexual. He reveals that he is a married man, but his wife is back in Athens. He rides me up the hill on his motorcycle, we climb into my hotel bed, make love without any fornication, and fall asleep. As dawn fills the white room with light, I see his dark tendrils are frosted. I make a note of that and continue sleeping with my Greek lover until noon.

Nicholas, nicknamed Nikki, works for the local Mykonos to Athens airlines. He has a wife in Athens. He does not work out, is uncut, wears the smallest bikini I have ever seen, has eyes as blue as the Mediterranean ocean, knows how to wear clothes, especially scarfs, is a gentleman, and he is infatuated with me for the rest of the summer. Sex is binary as he is bisexual: He is not capable of giving good head, but I can't satisfy his substantially uncut penis, so we just jerk each other off. No anal.

Nikki stops by the hotel every day to see me and make a date for the evening. He takes me to dinner at restaurants far from the hotel on the back of his Harley Davidson. I feel like I could lose my life on the ungoverned roads connecting goat pastures with hilltop churches and local fish villages. I drink more alcohol at these non-tourist cafes by the sea because I am running out of crystal meth, and Nikki, as handsome and considerate as he is, is annoying me because I am not able to meet any other prospects, sexual, financial or drug related, while he keeps buzzing around my residence at the Hotel Elyesse on his Harley every day.

Albin and Cyrus are my relief from the emotional sex games I must play whenever Nikki comes around. I go out at night with Albin and Cyrus to have some fun that I cannot when I am in the company of a closeted married bi-sexual like Nikki. I have limited funds, so dinners out with my American cohorts usually consists of me sitting at an outdoor table drinking water while Cyrus and his latest young intellectually stimulating conquest dine on the specialty of the house, and Albin orders drinks a salad, worrying about the quality of the water used to rinse the lettuce. It is amusing to think that a Greek waiter would try to understand the dynamics of our foursome. Who's with who? When I am out with Nikki, it is obvious to the people who attend to our table what the deal is. Nikki orders what the kitchen is known for, I order a vodka and tonic, times four before the first course of Nikki's meal is finished. I don't have an appetite for solid food, so Nikki calls for a check to cut me off from any more alcohol, pays the bill, tips, and walks me to the Harley. I have never been such a prima donna, especially given that I am over 40-years-old. But once a hustler, always a hustler. And Nikki is easy on the eye and locally knowledgeable of discreet beaches and cafes that only his vocation as a travel agent with a motorcycle could have. Nikki provided me the entitled experience of Mykonos only an experienced hustler could procure.

It is not always fun. I feel like I was given a tempting amount of alcohol at discreet cafes Nikki treated me to, but not enough to be euphorically wasted. Nikki takes me back to the hotel so he can go back to work at the airport, making sure that visiting vacationers are directed to the right hotel. He is good at his job. There is a science to determine-ing where someone would be happiest 1-14 days in Mykonos, and Nikki is skillful at that.

He knows I belong in my exclusive nest at the farthest end of the gay hotel on the hill, and I made all the arrangements myself. Nikki can park his Harley discreetly behind the hotel trash cans to prevent villagers from making assumptions about his whereabouts, like parking his Harley at the limited parking space for the gay Hotel Elysée every day around siesta time. Bisexuals are confusing. He is enamored by me, but more cautious of the repercussions of local gossip regarding his devotion to me.

I took beautiful digital images of Nikki poolside with his tousled streaked hair, intense blue eyes, warm smile, jeans jacket with colorful local scarfs around his slender neck. I tweak the colors from my downloaded images on my laptop with the white cotton canopy covering me from the intense orange Mediterranean sun, and the artic blue ocean beyond. On my Photoshop application, he is a brilliant Van Gogh painting. I'm not sure if my attraction to him is based on his visual beauty as much as the idea that I am stealing time and money from his Greek wife back in Athens. We don't discuss her, but I feel like I am acting like the 'other woman' disrupting a legally married couple. Only I am a man, and I am older than both Nikki and his legal wife by 10 years.

I'm comparable to the incomparable character played by Ann Bancroft in the Graduate. I've met Anne Bancroft. I went to her upper East side residence in NYC that she shared with Mel Brooks and her family in 1978, when I was going out on the town with a friend who knew the acting couples' 19 year-old son, who insisted we come over to his home while he and my friend and I ingested chemicals and alcohol in preparation to conquer the front door of the newly reigning disco in NYC, Xenon, replacing Studio 54 temporarily. I did not meet Mr. Brooks, but was aware of his presence when Mrs. Brooks announced to her husband in a tall, authoritative voice that their party-friendly son was receiving two young men as his peers in his closed bedroom before we stepped out into the adult night world of NYC. This is not Hollywood. But I was in the domestic NYC apartment of two highly respected stars, about to embark on a night of debauchery, after a standard parental introduction and farewell. The normalcy humbled me from thinking stars live any differently than the general public.

One day in Mykonos, Cyrus, the ever-commanding tour guide, convinced Albin and I that we should travel to the other side of the otherwise uncivilized island of Mykonos to the infamous gay nude party beach Paradiso, translated into Paradise. There was an easy way to get there, for a price, and a difficult way, depending on your budget. Twenty years ago, my young lover and I took the easiest way; a ferry directly from the harbor of Mykonos to Paradiso Beach. A picturesque as well as time efficient choice. It did not seem expensive to us 20 years ago. In fact, we bought the same ticket and took the same route numerous times, almost daily, in the three weeks we were vacationing in Mykonos. We had good paying jobs at the time, and Mykonos was not nearly as expensive as it was when I went twenty years later. The second method was to take a local bus from the same busy center of town, depart at a neighboring beach to Paradiso, and wait to catch the same ferry as it made a stop for departures and arrivals before arriving at Paradiso. The third was to take the same local bus to the neighboring beach, and hike the remainder of the way to Paradiso along a rough

CHRISTOPHER DUQUETTE

roadway, and over a steep hill up and over many large rock land division barriers for a sweaty hour before seeing Paradiso beach below already reflecting a hot sexual intensity with a clear blue bay, a beach heavily populated with deeply tanned nude gay German men exposing over-sized uncut sausages, most shaved and adorned with piercing and metal cockrings, relaxing in the sun like the dachshund breed of dogs resting in their masters groins. There were also pay for gay English vacationers with either protected pale complexions or dangerously uncomfortable burns in shades of pink and red. Finally, there were the Greek men, some gay, some not, some hard to tell, frolicking and posing comfort-able in their native land. But Albin, Cyrus and are were still fully cloth-ed, with knapsacks of towels, books, lotions, and cheap lunch provisions with still a half hour of descending the dangerous path before arriving at the beach level.

Some of the ancient stone walls that were built to demark land divi-sions were composed of small rocks and large rocks. The land was craggy with no trees or bushes, just dry dirt and short grass-like cover and stones. Those that were not half buried into the land were all but used to build the wall impediments. One such wall was built of such large rocks that the three of us able bodied but otherwise lazy and cheap Americans had to struggle to hoist ourselves up the large rocks, chal-lenged to walk along the summit of the rock wall towards the steep cliffs to the crashing ocean before scaling off the rocks to the land where the path continued to Paradiso beach. I followed Albin and Cryus up the rock wall. I was wearing a smart pair of orange and blue flip flops that were not produced by a renowned international sportswear company for hiking, but just an esthetically pleasing pattern designed by Barney's, the NYC trendy fashion clothes store. I liked that they were comfortable and unique. I also had on a pair of very baggy Abercrombie and Fitch cargo pants that flapped reminiscent of the green elephant bellbottom pants with 2- inch cuffs that I wore with a large green clip-on bowtie to my Freshman Hop in 1973. The bellbottoms of my cargo pants were so low and wide that they encompassed my feet, making it difficult to see where my flip-flops were securely placed. I was laughing and talking and balancing myself with the grace of a high wire walker when my pants caught on my flip-flops, sending me into a trip that I was not sure how I was going to get out of uninjured or dead. Albin and Cryus had turned around to witness my perilous dive from the 10-foot high rock wall to the green ground sprinkled with imbedded rocks below that slanted steeply down to the cliff edge to the crashing ocean below. I was blessed to land grounded on my flip-flop feet, skipped along about 5 hard paces without stepping onto any rocks, and continued to break my momentum hard to stop the increasing inertia of physics that wanted me to lose my standing balance and start rolling, or maybe even handstand with my prepared outstretched arms down the embankment. I broke hard on the fifth and final lunge and stood upright with my hands in the air in victory like I had just made a perfect departure from the parallel bars like a confidently trained gymnast. I was surprised that my fashionable flip-flops had stayed on my feet, which the balls of were throbbing from the pressure of landing very hard and produced bruises the next few days from the acrobatic impact from the fall. I was a bit high from the experience, not inebriated, but adrenaline induced. I could have pushed the large rock that I fell from its resting position and allowed it to roll into the ocean below, like my fate was supposed to bring me to death by loss of control. I attribute my survival to the grace my body acquired from a lifetime of strength training in the gym, and dancing acrobatically in discos for twenty years. Albin and Cyrus were more stunned and still afraid then I was. The three of us continued the last 30-minute hike to Paradiso, weary that anyone had witnessed my spectacle from the beach. We wondered and feared that a rescue helicopter would have had to be dispatched to locate my broken body. Not the entrance to a gay beach Paradiso that we would have been proud of.

The three of us perspiring Americans felt like we came late to a party when we finally arrived at Paradiso beach. Everyone ignored us. I immediately dropped my clothes and dashed into the inviting water for a swim, and got all the attention I craved for as I emerged from the refreshing clear salt water of Paradiso with my muscled pumped and enhanced by the vigorous swim I've always believed is nature's ultimate full body workout. Breathing heavily as I gracefully emerged from the water I always identify with the iconic moment when Bo Derek emerges from a coastal resort featuring tightly braided hair in the movie "10." I am always on camera. I know how to get attention. And every asset that made me the center attention I acquired from my street savvy mentors that I worked with at the Gaiety Burlesque Theater.

Other than partaking in a cocktail with Albin at the concession stand that overlooked the beach and provided a hot tub for the amusement of the narcissistic guests, I took advantage of my last bump of crystal meth, swallowed my cocktail, and made a spectacle of myself in the hot tub. The rest of our day at Paradiso beach was uneventful. We struggled back along the same path to the bus at the next beach and back to our respective accommodations after a long, strenuous day. I made sunset happy hour at my hotel and prepared for dinner alone in the hotel.

Each week I needed to pay for my projected stay for my room in Hotel Elysée, and each time I had to call American Express to approve the hefty charge as I was late on my last monthly bill that needed to be paid in full. But by explaining that I was on location for work from my Williamsburg, Brooklyn based production company BurgShoot, Inc., and promising that I would be able to pay my business card in full once I returned to America and was paid for the work I was performing. All bogus. It was easy to lie when I was desperate and high.

One night I went out to dinner with Nikki and was dropped off in the center of town to visit a bar that most gay men touched base with once in the night. A pickup bar. Nikki bailed out of continuing into the night with me as he was tired, had work the next day, and did not care to go out or be seen in the gay bars or clubs with or without me. I entered the bar, saw some familiar faces (Albin and Cyrus had left Mykonos to continue cruising amongst the other Greek islands). There was the well-built Greek man who I had never gotten closer to then the length of the pool at Hotel Elysée. I wanted to meet him. I wanted to talk with him. I wanted to take him back to my room and have sex with him. As much arrogance I was capable of exuding to the general public, I was always insecure about approaching an object of my desire as I did not handle rejection very well. But this seemed like destiny. And also, my last chance. I introduced myself.

His name was Servos. He confessed that he had been studying me for the past three weeks as I entertained Nikki poolside at the Hotel. He has been working various jobs to pay his way through the summer in Mykonos. Servos suggested we leave the intimate bar and the company he was keeping, an English traveler who could not compete with me for this muscular Greek Adonis' company. Servos agreed that he would like to spend the night with me in my room at Hotel Elyesse, only he needed to make a pit stop at his home not far away. His beat-up old economy car battered its way along rough unpaved roads past my hotel and into the dark hills of Mykonos. We pulled up to a house more battered and ancient than the car, the headlights remaining on as a flashlight to make our way to the front porch and inside the one-story structure. There is no one home but a pit bulldog, who seemed lonesome for affection from Servos as well as from me. Servos rummaged around his bedroom, finds what he wants, and signals for me to leave the dilapidated house for his car with the lights still on, illuminating the starkness of the Mykonos landscape far from the quaint look of the hotel district offering views of the busy Mykonos harbor. We traveled at breakneck speed back to the Hotel Elysée. Servos is nervous about parking his car so it will not be identified by hotel staff, so I suggest he park behind the garbage cans, like Nikki parks his bike.

I am surprised by Servos' apprehension about visiting my room in the Hotel Elyesse after we had the chance to get intimate at his dilapidated home, or even at some local beach, but it is so much more comfortable where I have been staying, what with the room service, view, stereo, and other amenities. Servos produces a plastic liter of Sprite, which he stores in my mini refrigerator, as if he counts on that product to quench his thirst while we make love. We have also been doing small bumps of cocaine since we left his cottage.

We explore each other's bodies, his being a good 25% bigger than mine, and our aroused penises, both amble in girth, his being uncircumcised compared to my carefully circumcised penis making for a more pronounced hammer head for a mutually stimulated fellatio session. The cocaine allows us to talk while we make love, asking each other about our summer experience on Mykonos, and what we thought of the other as we interacted on an informal basis in the hotel. I am surprised Servos is so humble. He reveals that he is studying to become a male nurse, and vulnerable as he claims he is insecure when he takes his Speedo off while sunbathing at the Hotel pool, only to eliminate tan lines from his hunky body.

After two hours of rolling on my fresh hotel white sheets, he declares that he cannot sleep with me through the morning because he is paranoid that one of the early morning hotel staff is going to identify his car and think that Servos is frolicking in one of the guest rooms, which is paid for by American Express, but that he should not be seen enjoying the benefits of sleeping and possibly eating the day away at hotel guest's expense. Hotel protocol.

I didn't put up a struggle about what he wants to do, as I am alcoholically tired from the long night out starting with Nikki and dinner. I see Servos to the door, tell him to call me the next day, even though he knows that Nikki comes around daily to dine with me. I have been stamped as a gigolo to a confused bisexual and renown summer employer to the island's tourist industry. I go to sleep.

The next day I wake up to find that there is no breakfast service, as all of the indoors as well as outdoor tables and chairs have been put on top of the tables, like last call in a bar or restaurant. It is the end of the summer season on the island of Mykonos, and all the hotels are closing up, boarding up their windows, and staff is anxious to get their final paycheck and return to their homes of origin and their loved ones. I was never informed by the hotel staff or anyone on the island, Servos or Nikki, that the summer season was over. I burrowed into a hammock and watched the staff frantically winterize the hotel while I thought to myself, where do I go from here? One of the staff that I am friendly with approaches me and confirms that the Hotel will shut down and close for business in 3 days. Nikki stops by while I am still on the hammock and asks me what my plans are. I tell him that I will check out of the hotel and take the ferry back to Athens tomorrow, returning to NYC well before I thought I would, but with no opportunities to stay. Nikki certainly was in no position to let me return to Athens to shack up with him with his wife waiting at home for his return, not with a new male American gigolo lover older than him, but with the profits he must have bankrolled living low in Mykonos while working hard all summer; i.e. no restaurant bills or bar tabs for two. I must undertake the long and tedious legs of the journey back to NYC where I have nothing but an orange 1973 Volvo Sportwagon in a garage that had arrears due before I could take the car out of the locked parking lot in Williamsburg. A car, but no home.

I don't remember what I did to pass the time that day, but I felt the war was over and I should return home. I saw Servos who passed me a sad hello as I was in the company of Nikki. I returned to my room to nap until Nikki picked me up for our farewell dinner.

I did not get drunk enough to be a happy hooker with Nikki that last night together. I don't remember dinner. He returned me to my room to pack for tomorrow's final checkout. Nikki was thirsty. He went for the mini-Fridge. He saw the glistening green bottle of Sprite that Servos had left. I had already taken a swig of this questionable thirst quencher and realized it contained Special K, Ketamine, a tranquilizer used to sedate large animals that gays and body builders use to decompress from reality. In the back of my mind I knew that the Sprite beverage was treated with K, now acknowledging that my last lover, Servos, had left the benign Sprite bottled tainted with ketamine in my refrigerator as a sexual enhancement. Nikki only took a swig, bid me a good night in my hotel room alone. We kissed, but I told him to go as I had things to do. Nikki left the room, I drank the rest of the tainted Sprite, and listened to Nikki's Harley tires chew down the hill to his apartment past the village. Was I demonstrating homicidal tendencies by allowing drug-free Nikki to put his innocent lips to the drug tainted mouth of the Sprite bottle that Servos had prepared for us to consume the night before to induce unbridled man-on-man sex? This drug was efficient and could have made pure Nikki on a motorcycle angling down a treacherous hill lose a lot of his ability to control the bike and his presence on this earth. He could have become incapacitated in a K-hole that would have left him and his bike twisted against a large rock along the roadway.

I jerk off and fall asleep wondering how I will get off the island of Mykonos tomorrow. I do not have any cash. I also arouse some sympathy and concern for the possibility that I may be responsible for the welfare of the only person who showed me some decency. Nikki.

Nikki wakes me up the next morning with an egg and bacon bagel which I devour with orange juice. I ask him about his trip home last night. If said that he felt strange. I was gently inquiring if he felt the debilitating effects of the drug of the bottle of Sprite, I allowed him to drink from. Nikki conceded that he felt a bit dizzy when he left, but that he attributed it to his lack of sleep and his feelings of disconnect from me. I tell him that I allowed him to methodically drink the spiked Sprite on purpose, maybe just to see him lose control after tucking me into my bed. He is amused, flattered, and not angry at me for tampering with his welfare with just one taste of the tainted beverage. I get my two suitcases, drag them to the front desk, and checkout of the already shut-down Hotel Elysée with Nikki towing behind me. It is my third phone call to American Express asking for them to cover the latest week's stay in the Hotel Elysée, with bar and kitchen tabs included. The three-week total was about $4000.00. I convince American Express that I will be good for the full balance due on my card when I return to NYC from my bogus thriving business, BurgShoot, Inc. I must have excellent credit rating with American Express, who did not seem to know that I am already on default with all of the household bills and 6 credit cards plus the $10,000 that I absconded from Citibank, my sister and her girlfriend, on the home equity loan I discovered I had access to.

Nikki has borrowed a Jeep to transport me and my two yellow Samsonites down to the ferry landing where he buys me a ticket so I don't have to figure out how much cash I don't have to pay for the ferry that will not take my American Express. We take pictures of each other on this sober day, hotels already boarded up until next season in the background. The pictures he takes of me on my digital camera show a tanned, shaggy haired thin North Easterner, bushy eyebrows, a bandanna around my neck and a look like I just woke up from a long night's sleep in my eyes. I kiss Nikki goodbye and promise to stay in touch via email. I have $34 American dollars in my pocket, no drugs, two suitcases of clothes that have not been laundered in 4 weeks, and no hard feelings about Nikki. He was a gentleman to the end. I had to still scratch and claw to get back to NYC.

The ferry ride back to Athens is terribly depressing without drugs or alcohol to medicate the anxiety of how I am going to get back to NYC with no plane ticket, and thirty-something in cash for the necessary expenditures: local transport in Greece and once I finally arrive in America. I don't even know where I am going to stay when I get back to NYC. My cell phone is no longer working due to lack of payment. The ferry is much longer returning, making many stops for locals who are returning from summer work in the Greek islands. The ferry finally arrives in the busy port of Athens 10 hours later, 1AM.

While everyone else seems to exit the ferry with a place to go to in a hurry, on foot, on moped, motorcycle, or car, I don't know where to find a bus to take me to the airport, much less what time the next plane is out of Athens to a connecting flight to NYC. I don't even speak the language, and if I can't afford a cab to simply say "airport," I have a hard time finding someone who will even stop to give me the time of day much less how and where to board a bus destined for the airport in the hectic area. Even the local businesses, kiosks, vendors with outdoor stands, and restaurants are closing for the day, giving me no opportunity to query even those user-friendly locals for help. I finally get one young women waiting at what looks like a bus stop, who points out a fleet of buses back by the ferries, which are sleeping with only their interior and parking lights on, their drivers either outside conversing with other drivers, or resting behind the wheel. I sprint for the pool of resting buses as if one of them is going to awaken from its slumber, come to life with its lights and hydraulic pumps rising it to full stature like an elephant who was resting on its front hunches.

I study each bus for a destination that looks like 'Airport' on the banner above the windshield and find none. Most have single letters, probably representing paths that the bus will follow in and around the area: A, B, C,... like subways in NYC. I finally get the attention of a driver behind the wheel of a bus that is just coming to life, ready to follow one of the alphabetical paths. He tells me bus D will eventually get me to the airport, with no changes, but a lot of local stops. I get on bus D with my two tired yellow suitcases and pay the fare with no question, as it leaves me $20.00 once I arrive in NYC. I am the only passenger that has a suitcase, much less two yellow plastic suitcases.

Bus D takes me on a three-hour ride around suburban areas of Greece, maybe the whole country, before it arrives at the Athens International Airport. It is 3am. I look at my two once funny yellow plastic suitcases that have been riding on this bus, smuggled crystal meth into Greece, held my unwashed clothes, and they don't have a nick on them. But I think they look stupid at this hour. I think that grey would have been a better choice. I don't really want attention brought to me or my suitcases.

The local bus from the ferry harbor deposits me at Athens airport at 4am. None of the ticket counters are open. There are no departing flights until at least 7am. Travelers are sleeping on airport lounges designed to seat one with arm rests that do not move, so the traveler must adjust to the arm rests by either sitting sideways with one leg resting on two consecutive armrests, taking up a total of three seats. Or, slouch in one seat with legs resting on their suitcases like a footrest. I can only sleep in a supine position with a bed that fits my 5 foot 11-inch frame, complete with a pillow under my neck, so I can't get any sleep in the airport as tired as I am. I leave my yellow plastic Samsonite suitcases alone as I wander within eyeshot of them, which is easy given their vibrant color, even with the terminal lights out.

One-half hour before the indicated time the ticket counters will open, a queue forms with international travelers, not many looking like America is their destination. I join the queue for Air Lingus, to follow my crumbs back from Athens to NYC by way of Berlin, Germany. When the travel counter opens, the queue moves quickly, as if most passengers only needed to be validated that they were in fact good to go on the next flight to the destination printed on the ticket that they have been holding all morning. I always found this stage of air travel redundant as long as you were not checking in luggage, which most travelers avoid by packing all of their belongings into a shoulder bag, and a wheeling piece of luggage that the traveler believes will fit into the overhead compartment. I need to not only check in my two large yellow Samsonite suitcases, but I must purchase a ticket on a wing and a prayer as I only have a very stretched out American Express Business card to pay for this ticket. When I get to the gracious counter agent, a local Greek woman in her thirties, with little beauty accents, natural makeup, hair styling, and jewelry approved by Air Lingus to wear while in uniform. She listens to my story about needing to cut a business trip short to return from the Greek islands as my partner has fallen ill, insinuating that he is hospitalized with the last stages of AIDS. I have never lied so despicably in my life. But I must resort to the lowest levels of human decency to get me out of this predicament of my own doing.

She buys the story without my having to call American Express again, and I get a $450. ticket courtesy Air Lingus from Athens to Berlin on the next flight at 8am, to wait for the connecting flight to Newark airport. I have never lied so much in my whole life. Except when I denied cheating on my lovers. I don't worry about it, or how I am going to pay the mounting American Express bill, now at $4500. I am just relieved that I am finally going home. Like I lied to customs agents about my purpose in a country, I am anxious to leave by saying I was not working for a government, or a source of media, but only helping the homeless through a non-profit organization that I need to return to so I can secure funds for further assistance to the desperately needy population in the troubled city of New York.. I've seen too many movies, and I am desperate. I want to get home, NYC., as bad as it was when I left it. At least there will be $1750. in security money that I paid to my Orthodox Jewish landlord in Williamsburg, Brooklyn who made me pay the difference every year that he increased my rent from $1500. in percentages larger than cost of living rates due to inflation until my rent and my security were $1750. I need that money. It could help me land in NYC with something to exist on with my American Express now definitely defunct because I have no more stories to tell (hospitalization? medication? rehab?).

I check my two yellow ducks full of dirty designer clothes and relax in the comfort that I will be under the care of trained flight attendants for the next nine hours once I board the plane to Berlin. I stroll around the airport happy to be an American with a clean passport. My only entertainment is to open up the photo image of the mascot Pelican in the port of Mykonos on my laptop, painting his feathers a variation of colors from the Photoshop palate while I still have juice in my laptop battery. Virtual needle point. I don't have any food, but I make do with the men's room sink to refresh my face and hair, and drink some of the tap water. I know breakfast will be served on the Air Lingus plane as is flies to Berlin. I may also get some sleep in my coach class seat.

I sit in the departing lounge for what is not the last leg of my journey home, as I still have to struggle with US Citizenship processing, baggage claim, the monorail to the NJ Path train, and subway to where ever I can find an apartment to crash in. I beg an attractive bartender for a glass of water, help myself to some cocktail nuts and ponder my not so glamorous situation.

Trying to sludge my way home with no cash or credit to improve the pace or conditions is like a defeated soldier trying to make his way back home. There may have been the abundant resources of the entire armed forces to clothe, fed, medicate, entertain, and have the soldier's back when he is a fresh recruit entering the war with high hopes, but after the war is fought and all resources are gone, it is just the soldier alone limping his way back, at the mercy of any crumbs that may be thrown his way. And no parade waiting for him upon his return. And no recovery or sympathy for what he has been through. I felt like I fought my own private war abroad.

When I get out of the path train on 14th Street in Manhattan, I climb the filthy old subway stairs to the street level. I am home. Or at least I called NYC home for 30 years, before I gave up everything a month ago to head for Greece. I call my ex on the pay phone. Shary answers, is surprised and unsure of how he feels to hear from me, that I am so close by to his home, and what I want from him. He can't offer me accommodations, but he does invite me to come over to his place in Chelsea for 3 hours so we can get high (yeah, crystal, that he deals so he always has a quantity to share), and catch up on what we both have been doing the last month. He is my ex, but we still are attracted to each other. I call Williamsburg, Brooklyn, to the loft with many rooms that was my good neighboring apartment for the 3 years I lived there and am assured by one of out of my colleagues that there is a free bed. I go back down the filthy subway stairs to the L train across town to Bedford Avenue in Brooklyn, and think about how I must get my Volvo out of the garage I have it parked in with last and this month's rent due, that I must recover my $1750. security from my landlord, and that I am back where I started. I don't know what to do next but beg my way through the next couple of weeks to find some work in NYC, couches to surf from, and to stay alive. The holidays are coming. I need to convince my family that I need and want to come home. I don't want to be homeless on the holidays. It will be a humbling experience to beg to return to my home of origin after leaving, prospering, and now desperate.

CHAPTER 6

MY SHING STAR, STORM ORION

I LIVED IN WILLIAMSBURG, BROOKLYN, and had a car to drive me along the Belt Parkway, past the Verrazano Bridge, Coney Island, to arrive at the Rockaways, a belt of beach off Brooklyn that accommodated all of the cool beach combers of New York City at the Jacob Riis Public Park and Beach. This was the most accessible Atlantic Beach that could be reached by subway, bus, car, or bike for anyone willing to cross a few bridges. There is the St. John's Episcopal Hospital, a state psychiatric ward, perched on the beach. Patients of the lockdown facility wander the grounds in pajamas and robes to hook their fingers into the chain link fence to overlook the party of diverse people tanning, dancing, drinking, smoking, drugging, swimming and fornicating in Bay 1: the 'gay,' 'nude,' 'black,' 'Puerto Rican,' 'party' beach that everyone who wanted to have a long day in the sun with good music and good people-watching would crowd between the wooden jetty and the rock jetty of Bay 1 with a chain link fence keeping the racy sun worshippers at Riis Park Public Beach from the private community of homes and bored white residents of the town of the Rockaways.

I used to come to Riis Park Beach with a gang of party worshippers who would normally only be seen at night in clubs dancing. We would spend the whole day frolicking in the surf and sun, taking magic mushrooms, smoking pot, drinking Captain Morgan's Rum, playing our loud boom boxes tuned into the incomparable R&B disco of radio station WBLS (World's Best Listening Sound) while the psych patients hung onto the fence separating us from the mentally insane and them from the spiritually insane. Yin and Yang. I knew of a young dude from the Bronx who found his way to the notorious decadence of the beach simply referred to as Bay 1 at the age of sixteen to take acid and loose his virginity in one night. The beach was notorious as a lawless public beach where the party did not end at sunset.

I drove my Audi from Williamsburg, Brooklyn to Riis Park Beach one sunny Sunday to relax and catch some sun rays because my crystal meth boyfriend, Shary, had widowed me for the weekend. We would be thick as thieves during the week. But by Friday, Shary would be classified as 'Missing in Action' after he left work, leaving me and our joint plans for the weekend dead and buried. His love for crystal meth would always step between our love for each other. I felt I needed to bookend my weekend with some coastal sunshine, and a chance to put myself on display as the proud and handsome widow who has lost her man to the sea. I may as well have been wearing a black veil. I lay my blanket close to the shore, read my Vanity Fair Magazine with my Gucci sunglasses and brown Gucci bikini that Shary had acquired for me to look good as he worked for Gucci on Fifth Avenue. He always wanted me to look good, even if that meant he was not necessarily there to appreciate it. I must have made quite the image of the golden man standing at the shore of Bay 1 when a perfect specimen of a dark skinned man awkwardly approached me to introduce himself: Storm Orion was a bronzed African American Male with light curls of hair and hazel green eyes. He boldly told me I was the most handsome man he had ever seen. I told him that he should drop the green eye contacts and stop bleaching his hair orange. He explained that he was a singer, and a model, and the image, even the name 'Storm Orion,' was a stage pre-sence. I told him that he could be more truthful to himself and to me if he had naturally brown eyes and naturally brown hair to compliment his naturally brown skin. He did not need to be so light to attract me. But the sunset shining behind us onto the Atlantic Ocean and onto the sands of Riis Beach made him look like a lighter shade of himself. He was as golden as me. It worked for the introduction. I was smitten. He was the most beautiful man at the beach during that sunset standing eye to eye with me in the surf. I told him I had a missing boyfriend, but if he wanted to contact me, he could. Storm retreated to his blanket of lesbian champions who had coached him to approach me after they had smoked a joint to embolden him. And bold Storm was. Nobody had ever walked up to me after sizing me up and said what he said: "You are the most beautiful man on earth." I needed to hear those words because I did not hear them from my absent Iranian crystal meth addicted lover, Shary. It felt good to be acknowledged by a beautiful man on this sunset Sunday on the beach in the Rockaways. I gave Storm my number, warning that I had a boyfriend, if he were okay with this, and that I would like to see him again. We made a date.

I met Storm, without his green contact lenses, where the best facsimile of Paris, France meets Brooklyn in the Park Slope area of Flatbush Avenue at a traffic circle that will either race city cars through the track of highway making a circumspection of Prospect Park, or crash into the stage set of the Brooklyn Public Library where theatrical pieces of fiction from the library come to life on the curved steps leading up to the gold leaved curved entrance like a Roman curtain. There are burnished blue brass fountains with homoerotic men with large merman tails and harps fighting to preserve their small, contained marble fishbowls with areolas the size of silver dollars protecting their fountain in the median of the traffic circle. I feel that I am the only admirer of these larger than life men that bear the sexy musculature of the art nouveau period. Cars are jockeying at the traffic lights to either buy a pack of smokes or a paper from the Metropolitan Magazine Kiosks that fit in with the Parisian street theme, or the drivers rumbling their engines in anticipation of a possible hit and run over a Park Slope marathoner in training.

I stood by one of the historic Parisian magazine stalls while my Audi idled, talking on my cell phone to one of my nocturnal partners who is telling me to squash the date, get in my car, and drive the fuck out of Eastern Parkway before a dangerous African animal attacks me. The Brooklyn Zoo is close by, and many a spectator has been savaged to death by standing too close to the otherwise archaic means of caging these wild animals out of their natural habitat in this ancient and petite zoo. The Annual West Indian Carnival Day Parade on Labor Day finishes at the traffic circle each year, another example of the untamed becoming agitated by being kept barricaded by the militia police that cause someone, usually the untamed parade participants, to be savaged by the police captors in riot gear.

I should be back in my own neighborhood, closer to the East River where the Puerto Ricans are rinsing their black hair on the west banks, and my bohemian friends of Williamsburg are washing their feet in the on the east banks of the same river. My friends do not want me to get involved with a Brooklyn Brown Boy. They are not racists. They do not want me to get down with the Lion King who might threaten their time with me.

As I hang up the phone ready stand my date up, Storm appears in the traffic circle like a flume ride flushed him down from through the Soldiers and Sailors Arch at Grand Army Plaza. We could not meet at some coffee bar, or the front of his apartment as Storm did not offer me an address. The mystery was in the location he chose to rendezvous with me; in the middle of a busy chaotic merry-go-round of traffic, like all the drama that was spiraling out of control in my other relationship with Shary. Storm was wearing light colored jeans and a polo top. He probably dressed as if he were going to the Brooklyn Public Library. Studious. He may as well have worn glasses. But then those brown eyes, with their bushy black eyebrows arching with the gracious attitude of knowing how sexy he is. They are not the comedic bushy eyebrows painted onto the face of Groucho Marx, but the thick yet shaped eyebrows of a Latin film star like Javier Bardem using them to express emotion in a silent movie.

I directed Storm into my waiting German silver chariot, my Audi, when I asked him if he had ever been to Williamsburg, Brooklyn, and if he would not mind our first date starting in my silver steel square canopy framed bed in my loft apartment along the waterfront. He seemed receptive to this fast pace dating game, skipping the dinning, movie, and playfully charming each other as in other normal "getting to know you safely" first dates. I wanted him to see my bed. I wanted him to dance around my bed in the middle of the day with no clothes on so I could see his Panamanian penis pointing straight up to my twelve-foot loft ceiling. I had never seen a penis stand on end like a ripe banana to be peeled by my teeth. Eight inches from the tight nut sack to the tip of the Komodo dragon's head peaking from the not long enough to conceal foreskin. I felt like Caligula in my imperial bed watching Storm return from the bathroom, the only room in the otherwise open loft.

I was never a size queen, nor did I see myself as the one who gives oral before I receive it, but my conservative morality told me that I wanted to look down on Storm's serpent and smile real wide as I passed it between my lips. I was interested in sucking his dick like it was a Popsicle until I had drained it of all its juices. I had been with black men before, but this was more like I was Cleopatra charming her Asp. I wanted Storm and I to become good lovers. I did not care that Shary's Iranian thumb-sized phallus had been my primary obsession for over five years. I wanted to have an intimate birthday party gift, even though it was not my birthday. Shary was never around anymore. I now had a play date. Storm: my brown boy toy.

I tested Storm's resilience to me by paging my coke dealer in Manhattan to see if he could meet me on First Avenue and Fifteenth Street at a Citibank ATM on a Sunday afternoon to buy an eighth of an ounce of Columbian highly stepped on cocaine. To me, this was my way of showing Storm how much I wanted to lengthen the amount of time we would be spending in my bed that afternoon. Coke would speed things up in terms of spiritual intimacy, but slow things down with the sexual intimacy. Storm wrapped his Panamanian plantain in his jeans and accompanied me on the ride in my Audi across the Williamsburg Bridge, down Delancey Street to First Avenue to take out $200 cash from the blue and white automated transaction machine that handled my Citibank account payouts twenty-four hours a day. Bills could be paid by check and the mail, but necessities like cocaine required cash on the spot. Storm and I sat in the air-conditioned Audi for what seemed like thirty minutes when it could have been fifteen. I never liked waiting for a coke dealer to show up by my car parked conspicuously on the street with two anxious men inside furtively looking at approaching traffic in the rearview mirrors. But when I want to shovel some coke up my nose, and Storm is behaving like an agreeable intern trying to make his first day on the job as easy as filing rolodex cards, it is not as arduous. I would have thought that interrupting sex to purchase powdered stimulants on the Lower East Side on a Sunday afternoon first date would have put a kibosh on any more hanky-panky. But Big Daddy must have his cocaine if he is going to continue to enjoy the rest of the weekend. The Rat's Ass Coke Dealer arrives forty-five minutes late in his dusty maroon Lexus and I enter his rolling Barcalounger passenger seats in vanilla almond leather. The coke is stored in a custom hidden compartment below the center armrest that rises with a motor after he turns a key. I guess the cops don't know about this trick yet. Maybe it was a standard feature in late model maroon Lexus cars with vanilla almond leather Barcalounger seats like in first class rows on a Dominican Airline mulling cocaine into New York City.

My dealer must know I'm gay, but we still only talk about a beautiful Dominican dish that we both know. Mariposa is as a fun party girl who wears tight dresses and black heels. She likes to dance at the Paradise Garage with a lemon-yellow wig on her otherwise flawlessly groomed shoulder length hair, speeding and spinning on her own coke which she will never sell to me. My dealer tells me about how he takes Mariposa out to the movies on the Upper East Side until he ran into his own wife in the customer line where a major ugly public Spanish cat fight ensued. I take my drugs and thank him as I jump back into the driver's seat of my cleaner and more contemporary Audi to sit next to Storm, squeeze his thigh as a sign that all is okay, and that he is my new Sunday afternoon delight, like vanilla almond ice cream from the Baskin-Robbins ice cream parlor next to Citibank.

We return to the unmade bed in my "too much sun in the late afternoon" loft with less interest in satisfying our skin with our hands and dicks then in our souls with our coke and our noses. The coke makes us want to interview each other for our hidden secrets and desires that no one has ever heard before. There are no more pointed material of underclothing and sheets stretching for release from under the fabric. There is not enough blood coursing through our members as the cocaine tainted blood is pouring from our noses into our brains. We are now in the material portion of the date. Words replace touches. I articulate like a court jester. Storm does not need as much coke as me. He probably could live without it and is probably just being polite. He can listen better than communicate. I'm wondering if we are going to be just friends. The idea of returning to foreplay and the fruition of sex seems impossibly remote. I tell him all about my terrible boyfriend who is not here, but that Shary is terrific, and that we get along so well, but he does this drug . . . crystal meth. It is evil and a third wheel in the relationship, and I deserve to cheat on Shary as he cheats on me with crystal. If I ran into Shary in a movie line on the Upper East Side, I'd probably have a knock down drag out fight with the virtual Crystal, and spare Shary my fists. Storm is very sympathetic, and caresses my honey colored body, telling me how magnificent I am, that I am an Adonis with my tight pectoral muscles and golden locks of hair on my Olympian face. I no longer need Storm's ripe penis, but I do need his ripe heart.

It is four o'clock in the afternoon. My home phone rings, the machine picks up: it is Shary. He wants to know where I am. He misses me. He wants me to drive to him at his apartment in Chelsea. Storm hears Shary's voice echoing from the answering machine around the barnlike loft. Storm sees me light up as I hear Shary's sexy Iranian voice from across the East River. I tell Storm that I must go to Shary. I instruct Storm to dress and leave and take the train back to Eastern Parkway, to the apartment where I am not even sure that he lives. I never find out where Storm officially calls home.

I have to drive over the Williamsburg Bridge to cross Manhattan late on a Sunday afternoon as the sun is setting over New Jersey to be with my drug addled lover who has awoken from his crash coma in Chelsea since bingeing on crystal meth and probably anonymous sex in bathhouses since Friday after work. I must make sure Shary is fed, and that the last few hours of the weekend from our taxing weekday jobs is billowing over the orange sunset hovering over New Jersey. Storm will figure out where the Bedford Avenue L Train stops to get him out of this carnal neighborhood of loft pioneers who have nothing to do all day but do drugs and have adulterous sex. I will call Storm next weekend. He will always be there. Shary eventually tries to kill himself, then, overdoses on Special K, a horse tranquilizer. Storm will survive. I will call him when the coast is clear. He is still with me now and forever. He is my shining star in the galaxy, Storm Orion.

CHAPTER 7
VACATIONING IN VIEQUES WITH LUCIEN SAMAHA
MY BEST PERSONAL PHOTOGRAPHER

VACATIONS WITH LUCIEN WERE NEVER EASY. He was born in Lebanon, and worked for TWA as a flight attendant, which made him more worldly then my American passport could ever reflect. While I prefer vacationing in boutique hotels where everything is minimally modern white, Lucien prefers to take the National Geographic route. His intention is not to save money as much as a desire to explore the world at a grass roots level. The Japanese trip had shared a year earlier left me feeling like we were doing more sight-seeing when I would rather be clothes shopping proved to be frustrating as I could not fit into the lean sizes of clothing standard in avant-garde shops for the average Japanese man. And when we were clubbing or eating, I could not drink the Japanese ales as I was trying to remain sober, and Lucien was DJ'ing in the clubs, leaving me to dance by myself in the mostly vacant mini-discotheques. But we did save an awesome amount on the modest accommodations he procured from a hostel guidebook and navigating the tricky alien subway system rather than taking a taxi. One of the most important lessons I learned on my far East trip with worldly Lucien was that I must always wash my hands before I handled my clean penis to urinate at a public urinal, as my penis should be preserved as the most sanitized organ on my body. I also learned that Japanese men would line up next to me to ogle at my enormous by their Asian standards' member, not necessarily to stroke it but admire it homoerotically.

Lucien and I met through a mutual friend, an up-and-coming handsome clothing designer, Gordon Henderson, who introduced us, and, because of Lucien's perceptive photographic eye and craft, and my irresistible photogenic looks and ability to style myself for any moment, day or night, as a handsome wannabe model just living the life fantastic in New York City in and out of clubs in the 80's and 90's. Lucien and I became close friends. We were a perfect match: Lucien; the party happy visionary of magnificence, and I, the easy going humble and natural beauty willing to mug for the camera or get caught in a unguarded look in his lens, with crazy clothes I would own and wear and mix and match with some of his on some spontaneous test shoots around town, from Wall Street, the World Trade Center, Thanksgiving in Buffalo, and now while I am vacationing with him in Vieques, Puerto Rico. He will capture me in the most intimate and spontaneous photo opportunities in my speedo's as well as exploring the wild vegetation and diverse community of visitors and locals coexisting on the open-door policy island of Vieques, seeking a break from the cogs of the real world.

My vacation on Vieques was personally intended to provide me with a respite from the trials and tribulations of my relationship with my drug addict boyfriend, Shary. My traveling companion, Lucien, was more interested in investigating the last vestiges of unadulterated Puerto Rico. The beaches are gorgeous and desolate. Vieques was not known as a tourist destination. It has unwillingly hosted the invasion of the United States Army claiming authority over two thirds of the small island's property.

Vieques is an island municipality of Puerto Rico. It measures 21 by 4 miles, with an area of 33,000 sq. acres. Population: 9,400 inhabitants who live in the narrow, middle strip of land sandwiched between two U.S. large Naval facilities. Since the 1940's, when the Pentagon forcibly removed thousands of residents of Vieques, and took control of 2/3 of the island, the U.S. Navy has been using it for the training of U.S., NATO, South American and CARICOM allied forces. Not only is it used by the Navy, but also by the Marines, Army and Air Force. There, they conduct amphibious landing exercises, special forces parachute drops, close air support, artillery and small arms firings, naval gunfire support, missile shoots, air-to-surface, air-to-air, surface-to-air shootings, naval "war at sea" exercises, and surface, air, and submarine maneuvering and drills. Besides the eastern third of Vieques, they also use 195,000 sq. miles of open ocean and airspace for their training. In the western part, the Navy stores ammunition, which it both uses in their exercises and sells to other countries. Industrial chain link fences with barb wire surround the US compounds at the eastern and western tips of the island, keeping visitors from the naval secrets and beautiful coastal beaches that are behind them. The US took territorial control of a domain that was and still is not acknowledged as part of the 50 United States of America.

After landing at San Juan International Airport, Lucien and I took a local bus to the South-Eastern most tip of Puerto Rico where a busy port accommodated our ferry service to the island of Vieques. We were surrounded by sailors, fishermen and locals commuting between the islands with their wares: chickens in crates, fruits, vegetables, breads, and eggs from the mainland unobtainable on the islands. It was over an hour on the primitive ferry ride to Vieques. Most international travelers would have taken a plane to jitney to Vieques from San Juan International Airport. Lucien wanted to arrive absorbing the local grass roots of the island. I was game for the ride as I trusted and admired Lucien's devotion to experiencing the high-end as well as the low-end of travel. If I were traveling with a lover and/or a less experienced world traveler, I would have insisted on more concrete plans, reservations, a final destination, a good room waiting for me with all the amenities I don't have in my New York City apartment. I always thought vacations should be luxurious experiences.

We deported the ferry in the harbor of Vieques around 3pm. We seemed to be the only travelers on the ferry and were now left with the struggle of securing transportation to a hostel-like hotel on the beautiful coastal side of the island, away from the only busy portal of the Vieques, the harbor. We found a cab with Lucien orchestrating the trip with his basic flight-attendant Spanish and the local driver's pidgin English. I guess it was obvious from the looks of Lucien and I that we were destined for the beautifully and simply named Blue Beach, where the beautiful people flocked to, with the Blue Atlantic Ocean surf washing up on the bright white sand of a uncivilized, unsupervised and unblemished beach.

We arrived in no time at what looked like a two level house/hotel with balconies on both levels, and eight separate apartments: four in front facing the street with two levels of balcony, four in back with no balcony, facing the rural hills and rooster coops that contained beautifully colored and long feathered exotic birds who would wake us up a dawn each of the five mornings we were staying there. There are pricier and chicer and rustic hotels and cabanas for rent on the Blue Beach front, but Lucien secured a reasonably cheap deal with the hotel's maternal mother of the family that caretake the hotel. Our room is on the second floor in the back, has twin beds and an efficiency kitchenette, private bath, and two white plastic oscillating floor fans to point at our beds as we sleep at night. Lucien takes a picture of me the second night in the hostel while I am reading in the white mixed cotton sheets on my twin bed, in boxers, with white toothpaste spotting my titanic sized pectoral muscles and my strong Scottish face to dry the mosquito bites I obtained from the previous night sleeping in this room that does have window screens, but still can't prevent the blood seeking pests from finding my virgin blood under my fair freckled skin. I learned the toothpaste trick from watching a VH-1 special on young top model Naomi Campbell in the 80's, confessing her beauty regimen. She would apply toothpaste at night to combat blemishes. I could sell the image Lucien took of me in Vieques to Colgate to expand the demand for their product: Toothpaste dries mosquito bites and blemishes as well as clean your teeth.

The 1994 Gay Olympics games took place in New York City, New York, from June 18 - 25, 1994. It is only late May 1994 while I am vacationing in Vieques, but I am training to compete in the Triathlon. My first and my last attempt to showcase my athleticism for fun and to be out and proud in this important first-time international event in the city that I call home. I get up from my white toothpaste encrusted pod in the hostel in Vieques, done my running gear (running shorts with flaps on the side to breath, New Balance sneakers, no shirt, and a ban-dana to mop up my bushy cinnamon locks), and take to the outdoor cement and decorative concrete block stairwell up one flight to a barren flat rooftop of the modest hostel. The roof barren of any furniture and is painted a protective silver. There are only TV antennas, and no protective ledge to make it safe to see over the top of the hotel property trees providing a view of the beach and the Atlantic Ocean cresting wave after wave over beautiful Blue Beach's white sand. I stretch my legs, do some scissor kicks for my hamstrings, calves, abs and core, some pushups to secure my pecs and shoulders and triceps from losing their natural and beefy definition before I start my five mile adventure run up the road opposite of the direction Lucien and I arrived from the harbor. I ascend a strong hill and find myself on a plateau of road hovering over a high cliff overlooking the Atlantic Ocean hundreds of feet below.

As I am running (I've past the threshold of jogging) minding my own spiritual and endorphin high business, when a jeep-like vehicle drives toward me with two gentlemen, who decide to stop and engage in a conversation with me. I don't think I am being cruised or picked-up, but they seem to be curious and interested in who I am. They are local to the island, and I am fresh meat. These American born Caucasian gentlemen are bronzed from living in this tropical paradise: Brian Nutley and his partner Robert Burges are rugged heterosexual-looking homosexual men who have fallen in love with Vieques and have committed their life to living there by building an exquisite hotel with open-air spaces and shades of thin silk fabric flowing in the ocean breeze to keep the sun out of the common area where quests are noshing on fresh local fruit and breads with tropical flowers like parrots on trees observing the gluttony of human nature on display. Brian and Robert find out where I am staying, drive down to pick up my travel companion Lucien, who is inventorying his film, the rolls that have already been shot and what is to be shot today. All four of us drive in the jeep back up the hill to Case De Cliffs, Brian and Robert's Bed and Breakfast, to give us a tour of the coastal cliff property, the airy architecture of the 10 deluxe rooms/cabanas as guests are walking around in their stylish and flattering bathing suits with sarongs artfully attached to their torsos as they pick from the breakfast buffet and make arrangements with the concierge as to whether they will horseback ride, snorkel, or get a massage that day. I'm there with Lucien in the "come as we are" clothes we had on; I'm still in my running gear, Lucien in a flashy vintage tropical dress shirt, bowler hat, and his omnipresent camera necklace. We are welcomed to enjoy the open breakfast buffet with the guests at the luxurious Inn and get an ear-full on the expectations of Brian and Robert on their newly opened high-end and high-cliff retreat. Lucien and I are driven back in the jeep to our low-end, rural hostel with rooster coops in the back yard.

We rented the use of somebody's privately owned small compact car with no luxury amenities to tour the island: no radio, no navigator, no A/C. We rented it for a smaller price then a rent-a-car contract, with no insurance, and just a bunch of paper maps to find our way around the island. This arrangement was made by our gracious hostess at our hostel. Lucien was satisfied. I was humbled.

Lucien had researched a vegetarian, local grown produce commune on a sprawling piece of mountain land populated by large community kitchen tents, small private pitched tents, latrines, and hammocks populated by bohemian nomads. It was run and predominately inhabited by dread locked lesbians, and a few dread locked men who fit in aesthetically and emotionally with the rest of the female population. There could not be any kind of aggression or power struggle on this commune community. Everyone's needs were contained on the large piece of land, power, produce, poultry, meals, entertainment, recreational activities, water, outhouses, and showering. There did not seem to be any interest in enjoying the beautiful beaches of Vieques, or to arouse any sexual intimacy. Everyone seemed to be floating in the same Kool-Aid of easy breezy temperament. The few automobiles and campers on the property were idle, and only used occasionally to retrieve more guests from the ferry at the same harbor Lucien and I arrived at. The commune was called 'The Mother Earth Kibbutz.'

We drove to the commune one day uninvited. We were received with a bit of reservation from the commune, but Lucien's cool and unthreatening nature smoothed out our presence. I hung behind Lucien in his shadow as I studied the surroundings and goings-on with hesitation that I would not stay here very long, much less make any conversation with anyone as I felt my muscular carnivorous gay male physique was a bit threatening to the lean vegetarian inhabitants of the commune. We were invited to partake in the lunch, for a nominal donation, and invited to come back to enjoy a home-cooked dinner, vegetarian lasagna, at a later date, for dinner and possibly enjoy an outdoor movie; maybe 'Thelma and Louise.' I was the Brad Pitt character who would seduce and rob and escape with their money. Lucien and I came back for the meal but skipped the movie as the mosquitoes were a bit untamed up in the mountainside at night. I had enough problems with my own mosquitoes in the hostel where I slept each night with toothpaste applications over my entire body.

To counterbalance the grassroots level of cuisine and amenities at the 'Mother Earth Kibbutz,' Lucien and I sought out a Four-Star Inn, not the B&B our friends on the cliff ran, but a Spanish-themed Inn with outdoor BBQ dinner and Mache band all outdoors around a beautifully lit pool and patio with hanging vegetation and soft white lights. It was called 'La Casita.' The dinner was not as pricey as we would have thought given the caliber of the Inn's accommodations and the attire of the staff and Inn guests. We mingled around pre-dinner in our smart holiday downtown New York City attire until the BBQ and buffet was ready for us to self-serve. We did not stay awfully long. Lucien had brought his trusty Bob Damron's International Gay Guide to where homosexual men congregate, whether it be a gay bar, a gay beach, or a public bathroom. There was one gay bar listed on Vieques. We drove our borrowed vehicle away from 'La Casita' to locate a shuttered hut that represented the only gay meeting place on Vieques, a hut that served beers only when it felt like opening. I don't know that any of the local men on the island frequented the establishment, 'La Penga,' but we were not going to wait around to see if there was any human activity at this desolate outpost. I don't think more than ten men could fit into this shelter, and there were no bathrooms or disco balls to enhance the lack of raw amenities. I do not know if anyone who had read about 'La Penga' from Bob Damron's publication drank there, or maybe just lured horny readers against the hut's outdoor wall with a drunk local.

We had befriended a mixed group of Americans who were staying in the room adjacent to ours at the hostel, their room being in the front of the building with the common balcony accommodating both of our rooms and our respective parties. Two were a heterosexual white couple, one was a single white man of unidentifiable sexual orientation, and the fourth was a young black chick from Brooklyn, New York, who I immediately bonded with. Jezebel would read my palms and my cards for free after we all returned from a long dinner at an outdoor restaurant on the shores of Blue Beach at night. Most everyone partook in a lot of liquor while I stayed dry and sober on juices and seltzer water. Jezebel heard me relate the parameters of my relationship with Lucien, and the reason for my escape to Vieques to get a respite from a volatile relationship with my crystal meth addled lover, Shary. That was the motivation for Jezebel to give me non-professional and pro-bono readings to her new non-threatening and damaged gay friend, me.

Jezebel and I left the liquid portion of the long outdoor tiki lamp-lit dinner to return to the hostel where Jezebel procured her Tara cards for me to draw from so she could provide a reading from what the chosen cards told her in relation to the facts I had shared with her about the concerns of my love life with Shary back in NYC. She had already looked at my lifelines, and they did not look that long. The Tara cards I drew did not look good to her either. The future of the relationship looked dark and foreboding. She was right. Shary would kill himself in another 2 years from his lack of hope for his dark life, and I would lose my sobriety and begin the same spiral as Shary: crystal meth addiction, unemployable, financially bankrupt, as well as emotionally and spiritually. I would lose my family and friends until I would eventually meet the same fate; an accidentally-on-purpose suicide attempt that I would both fortunately and unfortunately survive. It was the last time I would agree to have my palms, or my cards read.

Lucien and our new American pals from the hostel visited the beautiful beaches by day and took a ride on a glass bottom boat to observe the fluorescent eels in the swampish regions of the island at night. Lucien took many sexy photographs of me lounging on the beaches, with native young Puerto Rican men walking toward and over and past my body lying in pornographic star Raymond Dragon's swimwear collection. One of the most colorful shots is of me hiking back from one of the forbidden beaches on the eastern tip of the island we visited by sneaking through an opening of the chain link fence closing off the US

Navy's use of the island of Vieques. Don't ask, Don't tell. Nobody took such flattering shots as Lucien.

When our five days of vacation were up, Lucien and I checked out of the hostel, returned the car we borrowed, and got dropped off by the car's owner at the local airport where we took two consecutive piper planes available on a day's notice back to San Juan International airport, where we did not meet up. We each took two consecutive unreserved planes ride back to JFK International Airport. Flying without reservetions was Lucien's idea of being spontaneous with our itinerary. The price we paid was that we could not travel back to NYC together. Lucien did not seem to have a problem with either of his flights. I encountered major turbulence on my piper plane flying through thick mountain clouds on Vieques and got the very last seat available on an overbooked jet out of Puerto Rico for Newark, New Jersey. Strangely enough, I encountered two of Shary's good friends from New York City who were vacationing in San Juan over the weekend, and they were quite startled and surprised to see me in San Juan International Airport and on their plane without my boyfriend, Shary. I explained that this was my respite from him and the drama that was our relationship. They seemed to understand. They knew Shary better than I did. I was ready to go home to New York City, but did not know what to expect when I got back, especially my unknown future in this ominous (bad vibe) relationship.

CHAPTER 8

MATCH GAME DEBAUCHERY

1976 WAS A MONUMENTAL YEAR IN MY personal life and the world around me. I turned 18 years old in May of that year, graduated from the depressing existence I endured during my high school years, when all I heard from the fictionalized media and what I discerned from my peers was that these last years in the public school system would climax with the classic graduation ceremony pronounced as "the golden years." My senior year was highlighted by only one shining moment— when I was awarded the 'Prom King' trophy. I was eager and prepared to emancipate myself from my home of origin in the homogeneous town of IBM-Land upon acceptance to SUNY @ Stony Brook based on my academic performance, Scholastic Aptitude Tests, and three minor financial scholarships each in the amount of $500. guaranteed for each of the four years until effectively completing my undergraduate certificate. I was already financially sponsored to not fail.

Freshman orientation at Stony Brook began the last week of August 1976, when I declared my independence from living "under my parents' roof" once assigned a dorm at the University. As important as that calendar year was to me, the United States of America was celebrating its bicentennial. But my independence took precedence for my self-involved desire to live life on my terms. It was the year I came out as a gay man.

Even though the program had been in production for years, it was the daytime broadcast of the game show 'Match Game 76' that caught my attention as the television program that alluded to an 'adult-themed' world of integrity that I became obsessed with experiencing firsthand. 'Match Game 76' was nominated for the Daytime Emmy Award for Outstanding Game Show in 1976. I don't know who won, but who really cared about the Daytime Emmys?

I was already mentored by the faux pretentious dance extras who populated the Saturday afternoon televised tribute to the latest radio tunes that were capturing momentum in discotheques in America and around the world: 'American Bandstand' and 'Soul Train.' I had been privately studying and imagining myself in the spotlight: dancing groovy, looking cool, and being the center of attention of an anonymous audience.

I identified and compared myself to the exemplary contestants on 'Match Game 76' more so then the so-called celebrity panel. Filmed in Los Angeles, California, most of the contestants that got my attention and encouragement were first generation members of the beautiful people who personified the splendor of celebrity by inhabiting in the state of California where more celebrities resided.

I had to compete with my younger sister for control of the programming on our large color TV on a stand with wheels that could have been mistaken for a cocktail table in our basement's recreation room. It was an annex for my siblings to not disturb the studied contemporary ambience my mother secured for adult oriented visits in the formal living room. It was the first impression my mother, very conscious of her stature in the neighborhood, wanted to impress on her visitors. The formal living room was framed for attention by an oversized convex picture window that presented a diorama of the perfect nuclear family as nosy neighbors strolled by. The basement recreation room was my siblings' domain. It was not on display to the general public.

My mother's executive decision to allow my younger sister preference to watch 'Mr. Roger's Neighborhood' over any program I was interested in lead to sibling rivalry, and I never won. My sister's preferences and parental devotion trumped my desire to watch 'Match Game,' which viewed by an older generation could incite an innate homophobic sensibility.

Before my obsession with 'Match Game 76,' I was a sexually confused young man determined to allow destiny to be my guardian. 'Match Game' was the best afterschool show during my troubled adolescents. The humor was cheap and tacky, like the set and the wardrobe, but it made adulthood, which I had put my hopes as the remedy to my confused sexual identity, all the more exciting and desirable.

I knew I was sexually attracted to men once I was able to obtain a copy of the newly produced 'Playgirl' magazine, offering my first unadulterated examination of a fully nude male. But I still appreciated and championed the female gender, whether they be one of the coveted A-list cheerleaders at my High School. I was more obsessed with the 12 entitled cheerleaders at large sports events and kept a safe boundary from the male athletes competing behind them. The finesse these naturally beautiful and graceful girls presented was the focus of my attention. I believe I adopted these confident self-involved cheerleaders into my persona. I was drawn more to their performance than the male athletic team competing behind them. I was nervous and awkward in the presence of the gods on the playing field, even if I would never imagine any sexually intimate moment occurring between us.

The girls I choose to 'date' and introduce to fornication (i.e.: 'break their virginity') to increase my status as a sexual stallion while in High School. Once in my dorm at Stony Brook, I hung the photoshopped images of the picture-perfect models exemplified in 'Playboy' magazine centerfolds on my wall as art and more male attention. I proudly hung on my wall the iconic image of the infantile celebrity Farrah Fawcett, pronouncing herself demurely to the world with her perfect body encased in a red full body one-piece swimsuit, her brilliant smile, and her perfectly coiffed full head of hair emulated by every woman of that era, referred to as the 'Farrah-do.' Almost every female contestant on 'Match Game 76' sported a facsimile of the flipped style, regardless of race, and form fitting outfits that expressed the modern sexy look of a California girl. The men who were blessed with a full head of hair were equally styled to be TV-ready with a part on one side and blown out to appear fuller than their mothers,' but shorter than the earlier generation of hippies. I'm sure it took as much time to perfect their coif with the device designed for men: a combination blow dryer with a comb, enhanced with men's hair spray to make them almost look like a wig. The sport coat and tie ensembles were reminders of the lack of good taste in men's casual wear in 1976. Sometimes less is better, and these ensembles flashed loud patterned atrocities suitable for a circus clown. Most of the popular men's wear designers were out of touch: Pierre Cardin, Oleg Cassini, and Evan Piccone.

Match Game in its heyday (1973 – 1977) was the most watched day-time show for four consecutive years. Charles Nelson Reilly, a well-respected member of the philosophical acting community in NYC and LA, minimalized his intellectual and witty role on Match Game as less of a game show and more of a social engagement. It wasn't a compe-tition for cash and prizes but a wacky leer fest that modeled the promis-cuous, drunken, risqué, gender-bending behavior of 70's celebrities for an unlikely daytime audience under the guise of being a quiz show. The snickering, lascivious ways the regulars interacted, always hinting that the others on the celebrity panel were more depraved or druggy. They admitted their own questionable behavior was more than confusing to my 18-year-old suppressed experience and interpretation of what was veiled by producers and editors as inappropriate for young adults.

The executive producers of 'Match Game' were not looking for laughs at the saucier questions that the writing staff did not stop from slipping in the occasional double-entendre-type question. Some words were forbidden by the producers more obsessed with not offending some of the old-school but high-profile sponsors, like Fleishman's margarine or Head and Shoulders shampoo. 'Match Game' contestants were warned prior to taping there was censorship of words found inappropriate and offensive to this small delegation of morality judges. Yet, the popularity of the show, and its choice of bawdy, progressive panel of celebrities, was depending on someone (the contestant, cele-brity panel, and even the studio audience that seemed to be the temperature to what the winning and 'suggestive' answer to spice up the show from the staid family studio audience game show for a danger-ous sexually minded adult audience looking for some excitement) depended on the progressive writing staff, some who wrote for the most uncensored magazine influencing young Americans, MAD magazine.

The cast of the panel of celebrity regulars always perplexed me. I had never seen or heard of them as contributing to the entertainment business as I knew it, but within a few weeks of regularly viewing the popular show (a game show? a comedy of debauchery?) making it fill the 4pm timeslot to those of us adverse to soap operas and the nonsense of the local evening news. The show was starting to find its footing as the host, Gene Rayburn, quickly developed an intimate relationship with the anchor panelists that were unique with their television presence. Brett Somers, most famously known as the one-time wife of the Grouchy man on the successful television series based on the classic movie 'the Odd Couple.' Some of the dynamics of being married to Jack Klugman molded her on screen personality as a gravelly voiced actress who had seen and heard everything in life, no matter how low, mixed with quick wit to always provide comic relief during otherwise dull silence to an awkward moment on unscripted television. Even her appearance reinforced her quirky character as a dirty minded old maid, from her grey hair to her oversized glasses. Her only reference to the entertainment may have been her short term marriage to Jack Klugman, but she became an indispensable member to balance out the dynamics and her spontaneous and unscripted comments during a broadcast that needed an outspoken and comic comment to what could be dead broadcast moment during a strict taping schedule that would otherwise be edited and cut to be filled with Samsonite Luggage promotions. Brett Somers will always be associated with the loyalty and longevity of 'Match Game.' If she were not kept on the regular celebrity panel, I would have lost interest in the show during my first year of independence and unjudgmental attention to a risqué television show in 1976.

The ideal celebrity to sit next to the chatterbox Brett Somers had to be a Gay man, of superior intellectual capacity, able to not be influenced by his neighbor on the panel, which was the contemporary version of the dumb gay character actor, like Paul Lynde, the outrageously over the top gay Uncle Arthur on 'Bewitched,' and the dangerously sexually explicit member of the 'Hollywood Squares' celebrity panel, was contracted to Charles Nelson Reilly. The man had much more theatrical pedigree than the audience would ever have realized, but he was a regular that could always be counted on to offer the most Encyclopedia Britannic answer that was way over the educational background of the rest of the panel, the contestant, and the studio audience. It is no wonder that he presented his celebrity on the panel as the avant-garde unique that was given leave whenever he secured a professionally impressive commitment in the theatrical community. He knew where his priorities were. It was not 'Match Game 76.' It was 'theater,' where his talent as a devoted director of stage classics was his reputation amongst those that misunderstood his participation in the debauchery of 'Match Game 76.' His permanent panel placement seated next to Brett Somers also put an extra innocent but intellectual insult to his archrival, bawdy bathroom humor Brett Somers, in a celebrity favored show. While Brett Somers and Charles Nelson Reilly were intellectually and physically the dichotomy of comedy and tragedy, the third anchor to fans of the show was the British actor/comedian Richard Dawson. He freely expressed his sarcastic quick mind which 99% of the time was the winning answer, but his handsome looks and charm offered the contestants and audience a sober choice after listening to the coupling of Brett Somers/Charles Nelson Reilly bickering which made any answer they presented as insane, not of any help to the contestants much less the outspoken broadcast audience. In 1976, the show's success and the obvious preference of contestants and the studio audiences of them more sane, user-friendly, and game show smarts of Richard Dawson prompted the network to be the audience friendly host of a new game show: 'Family Feud.' Richard Dawson kissed a lot of female contestants as well as executive producers' asses to be promoted from the consistently tiresome position of providing the winning answer amongst the other off camera celebrities on 'Match Game.'

Brett Somers and Charles Nelson Reilly were introduced to the live and broadcast audience as if they were a pod that 'Match Game' had created and gave the Artificial Intelligence to be the anchor of an otherwise unscripted and possibly awkward show not focused on the contestants, but the quick wit of the celebrity panel. Nobody had heard of Somers or Reilly before 'Match Game,' but after the first season, their ability to provide unproduced spontaneous comments saved the show from otherwise dead air. They were the predecessors of 'Will and Grace.' There are no bars to the protocol of a witty, heterosexually lost woman and a desperately lonely gay man. My oppression of regularly watching 'Match Game 76' was because I just KNEW that there was a form of higher intelligence involved: the daily barb exchanges of Brett Somers and Charles Nelson Reilly provided by the comedic pas de deux that was sometimes bawdy but never cheap.

It became apparent to my 18 year old mind before I indulged in abusive substances that television was providing me with evidence that alcohol / medication / nicotine was not only obvious, but with some investigation, became an understandable insidious dynamic in the level of outrageousness of the behavior during a facilitator's Master of Ceremonies job, Gene Rayburn, who could appear slightly inebriated doing his protocol job with a panel of comic and progressive celebrity's disrupting his tele-prompter pre-scripted and edited job. It was apparent as a pre-alcoholic teenager that witnessing a major TV studio program go into melt down mode knowing the contestants would be in the same attire, as the next, and the next, . . . a week of episodes were filmed in 5 days, with breaks for the celebrity panel to change their attire, and exchange coffee for alcohol.

CHAPTER 9

DISCO DIVA DONNA SUMMER RIP

IN 1976, THE MOST DEFINING YEAR of my life, I was deeply affected by the inauguration of Disco music and the Discotheques that I devoted my social, cultural, and recreational time participating at, and professionally performed as a paid go-go boy. Ultimately, I found myself still market-able as a 42-year-old go-go man when I was no longer employable in the legitimate business world.

It was the year 1976, when I was 18 years old, anxious to be an independent adult, when the worldwide debut of the song "Love to Love You Baby" featuring the struggling background singer Donna Summer who finally got her destiny in the limelight. She had acquired the opportunity to be more than a one hit wonder, with the partnership of the music producer Giorgio Moroder, to be crowned as the Queen of Disco, a featured singer advancing her career to star quality for the next four decades, only to see her livelihood cut short not by lack of popularity but by the invincible diagnosis of cancer. The announcement of her death on May 17, 2012, coincidently is the monumental anniversary of my birthdate, which will always strike me as another example of life's serendipity. Every year on that date, I humbly celebrate my birthday, but honor the passing of a performer who I was more devoted to then any other diplomats of the Disco musical era. Her reputation will always be renown as she moaned pornographically through a 17-minute disco copulation "Love to Love You Baby" produced by the genius of Giorgio Moroder in 1976, pioneering a new electronically generated sound that would identify the dance beat that emanated in Italy and spread across the continents eventually washing ashore in America to be labeled as "European Disco." It threatened the existing and expensive manpower of predominately African American R&B groups, like the Tramps, and the professionally trained orchestras that could and would follow their maestro to an accelerated rhythm to accommodate the disco dance rhythm, like the Sal Soul Orchestra. Donna Summer's performance in "Love to Love You Baby" made her a star in the burgeoning dance music industry.

It was her second album, "Love Trilogy" that won me over as a fan of the African American woman transplanted to Germany as an aspiring songstress, blessed with the opportunity to become a diva.by collaborating with Giorgio Moroder. I was so fanatical with the mixing of three songs that were produced as side A of the album of the same name "Love Trilogy." I hung a banner from my dorm room window that was above the entrance that contained the stone engraved formal title of Kelly Quad D, some forgotten member of the Supreme Court (Dewey), to be displaced as "Donna Summer's Hall" that I wrote on a sheet and hung from my dorm window without seeking the approval of Stony Brook University administration or the populace of the dorm. I was never confronted with any outrage as Disco ruled in 1976. Just like the introduction of Madonna's first hit "Holiday" and the rest of that album's playlist, I was a slave to acquiring subsequent albums of these two novices to the already well-established music industry.

But as unpredictable as Mother Nature, Donna Summer's third album "I Remember Yesterday" was a bit harder to embrace. Yet I played the distinctly unusual album until I got used to it, and now appreciate it as a brave experiment with her craft and career. The magic of music is that regardless of your initial impression, the entirety of a well-produced album releases an earworm of memory into your brain, a moment in time that seemed invaluable. While the ambience of "I Remember Yesterday" had a distinct melancholy reminiscing a bygone era of dance halls, it was a surprise punch to end the album with the iconic electronic mastermind of Giorgio Moroder and simple lyrics to create a song that did not seem to fit into the album but was the highest regarded example of electronic Disco inviting DJs to mix in and out and around the simplicity of the production, "I Feel Love." This song has the notoriety of being the only electronic/dance/disco song to be included in the predominately rock focused top 100 songs by Billboard Magazine. Much as I was infatuated with the first Madonna album, my appreciation of her product dropped when she released "Like a Virgin." Similarly, Donna Summer's "Four Seasons of Love" was a love / hate relationship: I played it continuously, studied the ridiculously corny over the top images of the singer styled like a dated Hollywood movie star captured in the lenses of the photographic artist Francis Scavullo. The album was so short after the Moroder/Summer interpretation of the Farmer's Almanac definition of the four seasons of nature that "Spring Affair" was needed to tack onto the end, re-enforcing it as the "hit" song, and to make up any hard feelings on the musically thin album which included a wall calendar. I found some of the "seasons" off key yet liked the format. But Summer's next album I loved even more than "Try Me, Try Me, Try Me Just One More Time" that obsessed me on 'Love Trilogy.' I genuinely believe her 70-minute storyline on "Once Upon a Time" should have been experienced as an opera, like the 'Who's' "Tommy." I played 'Once Upon a Time' from Track 1 to the finale, over an hour of drama. When "Bad Girls" was released as a single and then the album that it was featured on, I was no longer a fan of the awkward star entertainer, as Summers had been inconveniently quoted as denying any loyalty to her gay audience at the offset of AIDS, and made a very "unchristian" reference to the correlation between that particular fanbase and the deadly disease. While "Bad Girls" and some other album hits played on the radio, I had no interest in buying it or celebrating Donna Summer, the artist, anymore.

40 years later, I read an article that made me want to purchase the "Bad Girls" Deluxe Edition, which has changed my accord to the album. Even witnessing the whitewashed version of Donna's turbulent life on Broadway performed by 3 Tony nominated actresses after a brave and ambitious Broadway production by her widowed husband, Bruce Sudano, a guitarist the once divorced Donna Summer met during an earlier recording session. Donna Summer the Musical was produced

and received critical reviews and 3 Tony nominations for the actresses portraying the namesake of the production. But Disco never was received well by Broadway, and the show closed earlier than projected. The 3 Tony-nominated actresses that played three eras of Donna Sum-mer's life could not sugar coat the diva Donna's hypocrisy.

It was not such a stretch for Mr. Sudano to contrive and finance a musical based on his deceased wife's legacy:

The musical devoted to the story of Carole King, 'Beautiful,' was a financial success, and even after the early closing of the Donna Summer Musical, Broadway saw two more musicals devoted to the singing careers of two still living legends: Cher (Bono) and Tina (Turner).

I have now discovered the hidden treasures of some of the less familiar tunes that feel like they belong in the epic "Once Upon a Time" on the deluxe release of "Bad Girls." "Journey to the Center of Your Heart," "One Night in a Lifetime," "Can't Get to Sleep at Night," and "Lucky" are more stimulating than "On the Radio." I was growing tired and too set in my ways to try to keep up with the evolving Madonna show, as she seemed to want to satisfy a younger audience who was weaned on more contemporary sounds, i.e.: techno soundtrack and hip/hop/rap. But I was finally converted with Madonna's release of the disco inspired (and Summer/Moroder sampled) "Confessions on a Dancefloor." Even the harmless pop group ABBA's playlist was borrowed without recognition or credit by the clout of Madonna. But now, 40 years later I was buying and realizing the genius of "Bad Girls." Of course, the deluxe edition offers even more bonuses. I love the emotional orchestration of "Mac Arthur Park Suite," even if the core lyrics and music are not original to the Summer/Moroder team. And I swear I can still feel tension in B. Streisand and D. Summer performing the duet "Enough is Enough" knowing that the divas never even worked on the song together in the same studio!!!! They insisted the producers that those were the rules if they dreamed of this superstar collaboration. Hell, even arch enemies Joan Crawford and Bette Davies played well together to complete "Whatever happened to Baby Jane?" I wrote about being bitten by the disco bug in Times Square, 1976, at 18 years old. Homo GoGo Man: a fairytale about a boy who grew up in discoland has been in publication for 5 years, and after consistently high sales, my publisher graciously agreed to releasing my play on words of the species "homo sapiens" struggling to avoid extinction in a 2nd edition of that book that allowed me to flush out my tales of nightclubbing in NYC 1976-2004 starting out as a naive go-go boy at 18 and ending up as a go-go man at age 42. What goes around comes around. Donna Summer was taken from her fans prematurely on May 17, 2012, memorable as it is my birthdate, and I will never exhaust my stereo from playing her volume of work, spare the 'Christian' messages, as the Summer / Moroder collaboration was as unique as Dionne Warwick / Burt Bacharach.

12/18/2019. Just got home from seeing the Donna Summer Broadway Musical, courtesy of my generous and thoughtful mother, luckily before the suddenly announced early closing on December 30, 2019. performed with the original Tony nominated cast. Traversing through today's amusement park of Times Square to get to the Lunt-Fontanne Theater that was next door the Gaiety Male Burlesque, where I performed from 1976-1978, did not arouse any emotional memories as NYC is not the same forty years later. The audience at the Disco Broadway Musical was predominately tacky obnoxious heterosexual Caucasian, which incited my prejudice about the production before it even started. After 30 minutes of Donna Summer the Musical, I was no longer a fan. The story of her life was told and sold to the tacky obnoxious heterosexual Caucasian audience, not satisfactory to a gay man who followed her musical and celebrity career evolve like Madonna's. I wanted and expected and projected what her music provoked in a disco, not in a civilized Broadway production. The saving grace was my prejudices for the young Disco Donna actress Ariana DeBoise, outing herself before receiving a Tony nomination, and killing her role not as Donna, but as an extraordinary singer and dancer, always paired with a cross-dressed female during any full staged production numbers. Sorry for all the performers who dedicated themselves to this musical, but I can see why it was forced to close. Disco can only be experienced in a disco, or in my case, on my stereo in my home. I danced in the best clubs in NYC recreationally and professionally from 1976-2004, wrote about my overextended addiction to the disco bug until I crashed and burned from the excesses of the lifestyle. Homo GoGo Man: a fairytale about a boy who grew up in discoland.

CHAPTER 10

LITERARY REFERENCES

'THE BIRDS AND THE BEES' SERMON was never dispensed to me. I was forced to perform my own covert research to find the answer to the adage: 'what came first: the chicken or the egg?' I burrowed through my parent's private chambers, looking for any material of sexual content. With the desolate house to myself, I dug through drawers, riffled through closets, and browsed bookshelves, disappointed that my parents possessed no 'skin' magazines, no condoms, not even a book of dirty jokes. My probing produced no leads on the subject or indication of my suppressed suburban sexuality.

And then I found the Promised Land, condensed in paperback edition. An encyclopedia to every taboo my enquiring mind wanted to know: Dr. Reuben's 'Everything you want to know about sex but were afraid to ask.' The title was as trippy as Iron Butterfly's psychedelic song "In-A-Ga-Da-Va-Da-Ve-Da." My superficial review of Dr. Reuben's judgments provided me with tidbits that would ingrain my brain for life.

Of the few chapters that attracted me, the chapter on 'Homosexuality' indicated that homosexuals, that I was not sure. I identified as one yet, met in the bathrooms of bowling alleys. What they did there I could not fathom. All that my naïve mind could wonder was the large wooden bowling ball coffee tables that would hold up to twelve bowling balls in circular cutouts. Someone could get hurt playing around on one of these functional but bazaar structures.

One of my more personal complaints I had with Dr. Ruben's sexual encyclopedia was his curious lack of a thorough explanation on the subject of masturbation. No one had given me any instructions on this act-ivity. As much attention as I had given to my member and having carefully read the chapter devoted to 'Masturbation,' I still could not quite figure out how it was properly done.

My nana departed prematurely from my 'life story.' She represented all that was good amongst the characters of my biography. I felt com-pletely misunderstood by everyone but my nana. She seemed to 'get me.' Nana had squirreled away every image I had ever crayoned and every letter I had ever scripted for her. The less appreciative and less popular members of my Klan seemed to live forever. In my misun-derstood mind, my nana died far too untimely and unexpectedly. That is why I bestowed her with 'Best Supporting Actress' in the life-time drama produced in my imagination.

My Nana's effect on me has endured from nana-heaven. Her estate consisted of those relics that my grandfather no longer wanted to keep in their life-long New England home. Nana's remembrances were boxed, sealed, and delivered to my mother, her favored daughter. But my mom had no vested interest in anything old, used, even antique. Her modern flavor in homemaking grew fresh from the pastures of nubile suburbia. Begrudgingly, mom took delivery of these cardboard hope chests, leaving them stacked and unopened in the furnace room of our home. I was driven by a kinetic curiosity to plow through the contents of these boxes; the same curiosity that fueled my quest for pre-Christmas treasures.

The boxes contained an assortment of home spun kitchen aprons, both seasoned and seasonal. My mother's culinary skills were directed by Duncan Hines, Shake-n-Bake, and Bird's Eye. Convenience foods precluded the need for her to adorn any protective apparel. Nana's aprons were not my mother's size or style.

Wrapped in New England newspaper was a hodgepodge of mint condition tchotchkes that had sprinkled my Nana's living accommoda-tions: imposter Hummel figurines, faux Versailles candy dishes, and tasteless salt-n-pepper shakers. Object's D'art in the sixties ranch palace where I thought I was the prince in hiding were acquired from the S&H Green Stamp redemption center. My mom's predisposition for modern mass-produced decorating left no place for any of nana's knick-knacks.

That is not to say that my nana's mementos never found a new home. My first and almost long-term companion was a deeply spiritual Puerto Rican distracted from his own proud culture by mine: White Anglo-Saxon Protestant. Excited by my family's heritage and heirlooms, he absconded these pieces of Americana from my Nana's box of personal possessions to accessorize our folk-art kitchen in the brownstone apartment we shared. My first long-term partner, Eduardo, also boasted of channeling the spirit of my nana when he paid for a reading with a notorious spiritualist in London. Without ever having met her, I suspect he drew upon the blessed spirit of my nana from her aprons as they decoratively danced across his kitchen, hung from a funky flea-market wooden step ladder.

The most personally influential souvenirs of my nana's life came bound in thin, yellowed, mildewed, and trashy paperbacks that I rummaged through to get an idea of what subjects my Nana was interested in. These titles never made a list of publications to be reviewed for an intern at Reader's Digest. But it was these very titles, or their clearance prices, that must have caught nana's eye and end up in her library. Interest in these subjects must have skipped a generation, because my mother never cracked one of these binders. But I did.

The summer that I was a frustrated freshman home from college, between dives into our above ground pool while plunging headfirst into the early adulthood of my life, my immaculate mind embarked through the pages of nana's paperbacks. Whether they were hugely influential or just reaffirming, my consumption of these books would provide the basis of my being.

In real life, the actor Montgomery Cliff played one of the queer dwarves to Elizabeth Taylor's softhearted off-screen Snow White. The biography 'Monty' read like an un-survival guide to the fragility of gay life. Looks, talent, and fame are bookended with alcohol, drugs, accidents, hospitalization, legal actions, and early death. Complete with a centerfold of black and white glossy images documenting Mr. Cliff's personal life, my sexual antennae were especially sensitive to the candid pictures of this handsome heart throb frolicking in the surf of Cherry Grove, Fire Island. The photos were credited to a 'close companion.' I must have made a powerful mental note to one day check out Monty's points of interest. From the shores of Fire Island to the psyche ward of a hospital, I followed Montgomery Cliff's foreshadowed footsteps. The prefabricated format of this biography could easily have been transposed for the adventures of another icon: James Dean.

By the ripe old age of 18, I had been subjected to more than enough movies to distinguish between the pudgy mug of Doris Day and the glamorous ice-princesses favored by Alfred Hitchcock. Ms. Day's raspy voice and chalky white hair aside, it was tiring to never see her represent anything other than goodness. Perpetually portraying the single working girl much younger than the actress herself had set a precedent for Mary Tyler Moore. Doris Day's biography 'My Own Story' contained an appendix prescribing her grass roots beauty secrets for that 'girl next store' look. She professed to lather her body in petroleum jelly before slipping on flannel pajamas to produce soft skin. Ironic that most of her film close-ups required the movie studio to apply the same petroleum jelly to the camera's lens to soften her aging look. While I was becoming skin obsessed at this stage of my life, petroleum jelly was not hypoallergenic for my sensitive and acne prone skin.

Ms. Day's prescription for home-remedy homeopathic meditation would be to lie on the bottom of a pool. I can remember experimenting with this first introduction to meditation by lying on the bottom of our family pool all summer, purging air from my lungs, sinking to lie flat on the bottom of the pool's blue liner and relaxing into a state of Zen for as long as I could stay in there. I don't suppose my mother ever witnessed this, or what she must have thought or said to me if she had. Suicidal tendencies?

Grandparents have a duty to instill folklore into the minds of their grandbabies. I suppose I only acquired secondhand information vicariously through the ghosts of authors like Doris Day and Montgomery Cliff. But it did make an impression.

THE END

EXTRO

THE TRIALS AND TRIBULATIONS OF SURVIVING childbirth to succumbing to fatality from a fatal accident, disease, or one of the four major causes of death (cancer, heart failure, dementia, or diabetes) are unavoidable. But there are numerous adversities that we must take responsibility ourselves, to overcome, and advocate with all the knowledge, support, and spiritual strength we can muster.

This book recounts the dilemmas' I have found myself stuck in, like quicksand. But as a member of the homo sapiens species, we are all equipped with the DNA to fight or flight. I encourage everyone in a futile situation to remember that they can always use their cognitive powers to rescue themselves. Never give up. It is a matter of human strength that hope and belief in a destiny you have always dreamed up is still feasible. Satisfaction with the past life we have navigated should not carry the weight of regrets.

ABOUT THE AUTHOR

CHRISTOPHER DUQUETTE

I AM BEGINNING TO FIELD MY TITLE once more in NYC after a sabbatical in Rural New York to recalibrate from over technolog-icalization of my life; however, all things come full circle, and I missed the Big Apple. Currently, I hail in Jamaica Queens NYC and I am busily finding my path to the hidden niches of books, people, and readings . . . look for me throughout our great city and beyond in the 2017 – 2018 book-signing circuit.

If you have a venue, bookshop, store, grocery mart, location for a book reading and signing – I'm interested in hearing from you and so is my publisher, "Q" of DonnaInk Publications, L.L.C. who delivers quality creations, heartfelt support, and authorial success.

Mostly, I want to say I appreciate you all as readers who have traversed the Disco Era or heard about it. If you are coming out, in the closest, straight, and/or unafraid of life choices, or as gay as a blue-jay – thank you for being here and sharing this glimpse of history.

As a clean adult, post-era, I'm privileged to share a moment of history in recovery and pray the same for each of you.

~Christopher Duquette

2ND
SPIRIT BOOKS

Donnalnk Publications, L.L.C.

DonnaInk Publications, L.L.C.
2nd Spirit Books
601 McReynolds Street
Carthage, NC 28327
910-947-3189
www.donnaink.com
contact@donnainkpublications.com